STUDIES IN SOCIOLOGY

Volume 1

I0095066

A SOCIOLOGY OF
FRIENDSHIP AND KINSHIP

A SOCIOLOGY OF
FRIENDSHIP AND KINSHIP

GRAHAM A. ALLAN

Routledge
Taylor & Francis Group

LONDON AND NEW YORK

First published in 1979 by George Allen & Unwin Ltd

This edition first published in 2022
by Routledge
4 Park Square, Milton Park, Abingdon, Oxon OX14 4RN

605 Third Avenue, New York, NY 10017

Routledge is an imprint of the Taylor & Francis Group, an informa business

British Library Cataloguing in Publication Data
A catalogue record for this book is available from the British Library

ISBN: 978-1-03-207714-7 (Set)
ISBN: 978-1-00-321960-6 (Set) (ebk)
ISBN: 978-1-03-210363-1 (Volume 1) (hbk)
ISBN: 978-1-03-210373-0 (Volume 1) (pbk)
ISBN: 978-1-00-321501-1 (Volume 1) (ebk)

DOI: 10.4324/9781003215011

Publisher's Note
The publisher has gone to great lengths to ensure the quality of this reprint but points out that some imperfections in the original copies may be apparent.

Disclaimer
The publisher has made every effort to trace copyright holders and would welcome correspondence from those they have been unable to trace.

A SOCIOLOGY
OF FRIENDSHIP
AND KINSHIP

Graham A. Allan
Lecturer in Sociology, University of Southampton

London
GEORGE ALLEN & UNWIN
Boston   Sydney

First published in 1979

GEORGE ALLEN & UNWIN LTD
40 Museum Street, London WC1A 1LU

© George Allen & Unwin (Publishers) Ltd, 1979

British Library Cataloguing in Publication Data

Allan, Graham A.
   Sociology of friendship and kinship
   – (Studies in sociology; no. 10).
   1. Friendship 2. Kinship
   I. Title II. Series
   301.11′2   HM132   79–40290

   ISBN 0–04–301104–7
   ISBN 0–04–301105–5 Pbk

Typeset in 10 on 11 point Times by Trade Linotype Ltd, Birmingham
and printed in Great Britain
by Unwin Brothers Ltd, Old Woking, Surrey

Preface

Many people have helped me in the course of writing this book. Amongst the most important are the individuals who allowed me to interview them about their various sociable relationships. Without their help and interest this book would not have been written. As promised, their names and that of the place in which they lived have been altered to ensure their anonymity. Colin Bell supervised the research from which this book grew and has continued to take an interest in it. I owe him a great deal, not only for his help and encouragement but also for informing my general perspective on sociology. Bill Williams was instrumental in my developing my thesis into this book. His numerous suggestions about its form and content have improved it greatly. Others who have commented on the research and helped in various ways include Mary Allan, Diana Barker, Eric Briggs, Joan Busfield, Steve Chibnall, John Hall, Joan Higgins, Halina Jarrowson, David Kennaby, Sue Lane, Duncan Mitchell, Don Munro, Bob Paisley, John Smith, Peter Townsend, Sue Wheatley and Bob Witkin.

I would also like to thank Ros Thomson, Alex Granger and Karen Fulbrook who at different times typed all or part of the book with remarkable speed and efficiency.

Finally I would like to thank the publishers of the *Journal of Marriage and the Family* and the *British Journal of Sociology* for allowing me to make use of material first published in articles entitled, respectively, 'Sibling solidarity' (1977) and 'Class variations in friendship patterns' (1977).

For Richard and Nicola

CONTENTS

Chapter 1

Introduction

In one of the most-quoted sentences from any kinship research, Raymond Firth wrote: 'Kinship in Britain [is] pervasive, intangible, still largely unstudied, with its significance either not appreciated or in danger of being over-estimated . . .' (1961, p. 305). This volume has evolved from an attempt to add to the available knowledge of the significance of kin relationships in present-day Britain. As with all research, this task is more easily stated than achieved. Exactly what is meant by the 'significance' of kin relationships? How is their significance to be recognised and measured? On what criteria is it to be decided? There are two aspects involved in answering these questions. First, it needs to be shown that kin relationships have *some* significance in the way people organise and run their everyday lives. This, indeed, is what a growing number of kinship studies have demonstrated. But to understand more fully the significance of kin relationships in modern social life it is necessary to go a stage further and compare kin relationships with other types of relationship that common knowledge and experience suggest are functionally similar. In particular, ties of friendship seem important here. In this way some standard by which to judge the significance of kin relationships can be achieved. As Bell notes, 'we do not really know how important kinship is unless it is studied in relation to other systems of interaction, like those of friendship, work and neighbouring' (1971, p. 131).

But if kin relationships are to be compared with other types of relationship, it would seem inevitable that kinship *per se* becomes less important in the overall scheme of analysis. Certainly, as the comparative perspective of the present book developed, the primary focus shifted from kin relationships to other types of sociable relationships, with the variety of non-kin relationships that approach friendship becoming increasingly central. Concomitantly, the range of the comparisons possible between the different types of relationship was reduced, so that eventually interest centred on sociable interaction, be it with kin or non-kin, at the expense of the variety of other topics that are equally stimulating and legitimate. It is thus that what follows is concerned with analysing and comparing different types of sociable relationships.

I take the term sociable relationship to include all those that an individual enters into purposefully and voluntarily for primarily non-instrumental reasons. This is not intended to be taken as an authoritative and conclusive definition, but as an adequate working one in the present context. Indeed, giving a precise definition of sociable relationships is probably impossible. Various elements such as enjoyment of interaction, intention, non-instrumentality, lack of constraint, etc., are involved which do not necessarily relate to one another in any consistent manner. Thus while some relationships are quite evidently sociable and others are equally obviously not, at the boundary there are no clear-cut, objective criteria.

Take work relationships as an example. To the extent that one's work-fellows are not freely chosen but are interacted with because of the contingencies of work, the relationships one has with them are not sociable ones. To the extent that one purposefully interacts with them out of choice in a way defined as peripheral to the work performance, they are. As with the definition of leisure activities, in the end the actor's understanding is paramount.

It is in many ways surprising that previous studies have not attempted to compare other types of apparently similar relationships with kin ones. Since Parsons's famous, though frequently misunderstood, statements about the structural isolation of the nuclear family, an increasing amount of research has been concerned with analysing sociability amongst kin.[1] Yet very few of these studies report on friendship or other types of sociable ties in general.

This lack of comparative focus is not a consequence of the subject matter itself being unimportant or without theoretical significance. Changes in the nature of personal relationships in society have long concerned sociologists. Tönnies's famous distinction between *Gemeinschaft* and *Gesellschaft* was merely the starting point of a trail traversed by many since. Apart from Simmel, the contributions of those sociologists such as Burgess, Cooley, Park and Wirth based at the University of Chicago in the 1920s and 1930s have been seminal. Later writers, in disagreeing with the perspective adopted by the above, and especially Wirth in his paper 'Urbanism as a way of life' (1938), have emphasised the continuing importance of primary relationships and groups in our society. They have demonstrated that personal relationships do not simply provide compensation and distraction from the more 'serious' issues of social life, but that they are the flesh which covers the bare bones of social structure.

Thus for example Litwak and his associates, in their discourse with Parsons, have demonstrated the centrality of primary groups in industrial society. In particular they have shown how various bureaucratic agencies depend on the assistance of particularistic primary groups to deal with unpredictable contingencies (Litwak, 1960a; 1960b; 1965; Litwak and Szelenyi, 1969; see Harris, 1969). Other studies have shown how the networks of neighbourhood and work relationships influence the way people interpret and experience their worlds, and are thus of consequence in shaping political and economic aspirations (Whyte, 1943; Dennis, Henriques and Slaughter, 1956; Liebow, 1967; Bott, 1971). In England this thesis has been developed by David Lockwood, particularly in his well-known paper 'Sources of variation in working class images of society' (Lockwood, 1966; see also Bulmer, 1975). Again, from Elton Mayo onwards, research has shown that if organisations are to be understood fully, their informal as well as their formal structure needs to be analysed. In another area, Bernstein and others concerned with socio-linguistics have explored 'how symbolic systems are both realizations and regulators of the structure of social relationships' (Bernstein, 1973, p. 194). Equally, community studies have demonstrated how social status is expressed through, and symbolised by, informal friendship associations (Williams, 1956; Littlejohn, 1963), while others have shown the importance of friendship cliques in maintaining political power (Birch, 1959; Stacey, 1960). Finally, Lupton and Wilson (1959) have shown the remarkable integration of social and business life amongst top decision-makers.

Even from these few examples it can be seen that the study of sociable relationships is not just a peripheral interest in sociology. Rather it is central to its main concerns. None the less, it remains true that there have been very few studies that have attempted to analyse and compare the nature and basis of different types of sociable relationship. As with kinship studies, most concentrate on some small subset of them. The exceptions to this are the various occupational and community studies that have been published in the last twenty years.[2]

PATTERNS OF SOCIABILITY IN OCCUPATIONAL AND COMMUNITY STUDIES

Even though sociable patterns do not figure large in the overall concern of these studies, the differing content of the variety of personal relationships that people enter into with others is analysed more fully in them – especially the British ones[3] – than in any other body of literature. In the main, the interest of these studies in patterns of sociability lies in analysing the systematic differences that are present in the middle-class and working-class respondents' treatment of kin and friends. This is also a theme which runs through the present study.

While many of the occupational and urban community studies

only discuss friendship patterns briefly, taken together they show a surprising degree of convergence and all conform to a broad pattern. The general thesis they put forward is that working-class friendships tend to be restricted to kin, supplemented to some extent by neighbours and workmates, while middle-class respondents appear to form friendships with a far wider variety of people, and do not limit them to these particular structured categories of others. Naturally, this 'general thesis' is interpreted in a number of ways with, for example, the importance of neighbours and workmates in working-class sociable life not being agreed upon. In some studies the working-class respondents appear to have limited their informally planned, semi-organised social life to kin, with non-kin associates being seen much more haphazardly. These respondents were friendly with the latter, but did not regard or treat them as friends. In other studies, however, the working-class respondents do not seem to have restricted their important relationships solely to kin but include amongst their friends a (limited) number of neighbours and workmates.

In part such differences as these obviously stem from the different ways the concept of friendship is operationalised. (For example, are kin and friends two distinct sets, or can kin be included as friends? Is home visiting and entertainment a necessary criterion of friendship? And so on.) Nevertheless, all the writers agree that the typical working-class pattern is different from the typical middle-class one. The middle class are taken as generally having a number of friends who play a prominent part in their social life, but as not relying exclusively on kin, or even neighbourhood or work groups, for them. Friends may be neighbours, colleagues, fellow club members, clients or business associates, they may even be brothers or cousins; it does not matter. They are interacted with because they are liked as individuals, irrespective of the structured category of others to which they belong. Thus, contrary to the working-class pattern, middle-class respondents are seen as choosing their friends from a wide variety of others, with membership of the kin group, or of any other restricted set of people, being unimportant in this process.

These studies' analysis of class variation in friend and kin relationships is a central theme throughout this book. However, an important point which arises here is that the concepts of 'friend' and 'friendship' are treated uncritically in this literature. The category 'friend' appears to be considered equivalent to the categories 'kin' or 'neighbour' or 'colleague' in that there is no discussion of what makes a sociable relationship come to be regarded as one of friendship. As will be developed in a later chapter, this is inappropriate, for friendship is judged on criteria internal to the character of the on-going relationship, while the other categories are defined more by criteria external to it. The former label refers to a property of the relationship, but these latter tend to refer to properties of the individual in that relationship.

FRIENDSHIP AND KINSHIP

This book, then, is concerned with extending the analysis of sociable relationships provided in occupational and community studies. It examines the set of relationships that make up what has been called the individual's 'sociability network' (Edgell, n.d.). The focus throughout will be on the way that different respondents organise their various relationships, with particular attention being given to a comparison of the different forms of solidarity involved in kin and non-kin relationships. While this will entail looking at the proportions of kin and non-kin interacted with most frequently as well as the functions that different 'primary group structures', such as kin, friends, neighbours, (see Litwak and Szelenyi, 1969), perform, the emphasis will be placed much more than is usual on investigating the nature of the social situations in which people typically activate their different relationships. Its concern will be with the way relationships are developed and with what those involved define as relevant to them, for in this way their parameters and boundaries can be made more apparent.

The data on which this book draws come from various sources. While much of the content derives from an empirical study into patterns of sociability conducted by the author in the early 1970s, the book is not intended to be a research monograph in the traditional sense. Rather the emphasis throughout the text will be on consolidating our current knowledge of kin and non-kin sociability by critically examining the main themes and findings of previous studies. However, the arguments and interpretations found in the secondary material will be illustrated and, where appropriate, extended with the aid of examples, case histories and 'apt illustrations' from the field research. In this way, it is hoped that data from the primary and secondary sources will complement each other and result in a more adequate understanding of patterns of sociability than has been available hitherto.

The theoretical approach adopted in this book differs substantially from that used in most previous studies. They have tended to emphasise 'objective' characteristics of relationships – such as frequency of interaction, home-visiting and exchange of services – at the expense of the actor's own definitions and constructs. While 'objective' features are not ignored, this tendency is reversed in the present study. The theoretical perspective that informs it is derived from symbolic interactionism, so that throughout its focus is on the definitions of their relationships held by the interactants rather than on indices with uncertain significance imposed by an outside analyst.

More particularly, the standpoint adopted here calls for analysing the implicit 'rules of relevance' that the individual constructs for each of his relationships. While most people do not work out carefully and explicitly what is and what is not relevant to a relationship, it is reasonable to assume that any relationship can only continue in a satisfactory way for the actors because they have tacitly come to an agreement about what is to be involved in that relationship. While liable to change over time, the definition they have of their involvement with one another is likely to set the scene for their interaction and shape its character. Whenever sociologists discuss patterns of sociability, or talk of individuals ordering and structuring their personal networks, they are saying this, or something similar to it, in macro form. They are concerned with the consistent patterning in what a respondent defines as relevant to the sets of relationships in which he is involved. By analysing the rules of relevance of different relationships it is possible to specify the character of the solidarity they encompass and, consequently, to analyse their common and dissimilar properties. In this way the structuring principles underlying patterns of sociability can be uncovered.

OUTLINE OF THE BOOK

In Chapter 2 I shall develop this theoretical perspective at length, discussing the manner in which it differs from previous approaches. One difficulty here is that while the primary data could be collected with this framework in mind, the secondary material used in the book was not. Consequently, if primary and secondary data are to complement each other in the way intended, the approach advocated here is necessarily constrained by the perspectives informing previous research. The task then is to create a model that focuses on the way in which relationships are purposefully organised, yet is capable of adapting and reinterpreting the evidence of earlier studies.

Chapter 3 will be concerned with describing the research procedures used in the primary study of sociability mentioned above. As many of the themes to be discussed later will be illustrated by reference to material gathered in this study, it is important that the reader has an opportunity to judge the adequacy of the data collection techniques used in it. The chapter will consider the design of the sample, the social characteristics of the respondents and features of the interviewing process. In it the emphasis will be on data collection as an active social process in which the theoretical ideal is continually modified by the practical contingencies of fieldwork.

In Chapter 4 I discuss the nature of kinship and friendship, examining the way they are socially bestowed. Both, though especially friendship, are labels applied to others who satisfy certain criteria. Consequently both the variable and invariable features of these criteria need to be examined before people's attribution of the labels can be compared. The components of friendship as a form of relationship have received rather less attention in the previous literature than those of kinship, so I shall concentrate more heavily on them, examining what it is about the way non-kin sociable relationships are organised and structured that makes the term 'friend' suitable or otherwise. As I have implied above, most empirical studies of friendship tend to ignore the determinants of this labelling process. They treat friendship uncritically as though it were 'natural' and not a social construction involving specifiable principles of organisation.

In Chapters 5 and 6 the way non-kin relationships are organised will be examined. As noted earlier, all previous studies have reported that the basic division in their organisation is a class based one with the middle class having rather more friends than the working class. A central theme in this book will be that more than anything this is a consequence of the diverse form in which non-kin relationships are constructed. Both in order to demonstrate this and to make the best use of previous research, middle- and working-class non-kin relationships will be dealt with separately. Chapter 5 will discuss the former while Chapter 6 will consider the latter. The differences in the two groups' sociable patterns will be related to differences in their material circumstances and, in addition, the consistency of these patterns with other aspects of middle-class and working-class culture will be illustrated.

Chapter 7 analyses kin relationships, concentrating on primary kin as these are the most important in people's patterns of sociability. The importance for kinship organisation (and ideology) of genealogies being social networks, in the fullest sense of this maligned term, will be examined, as will differences in male and female, middle- and working-class kin relationships. The chapter will also compare kin relationships with the non-kin ones discussed in the previous chapter, and will examine why kin relationships tend to persist despite a relatively low exchange content while non-kin ones tend not to.

In Chapter 8, patterns of sociability will be considered as a whole. The various forms of sociable relationship discussed previously will be pieced together to provide an overview of them all. The important task of this chapter is to complement the voluntaristic stance of the earlier chapters by examining the structural determinants of sociable networks as on-going systems of relationships.

The final chapter will summarise the main conclusions of the preceding chapters, relating them to the wider context of previous research in the fields of community and family sociology. It also returns to a consideration of some of the issues raised in this chapter, especially those concerning the nature and functioning of primary groups in modern industrial society.

NOTES: CHAPTER 1

1 For Britain, cf.: Shaw (1954); Firth (1956); Rosser and Harris (1961, 1965); Young and Willmott (1962); Townsend (1963); Williams (1965); Bell (1968a, 1968b); Firth, Hubert and Forge (1970). The American literature on sociability between kin is immense, though in the present context Adams's contributions are amongst the most important. Sussman and Burchinal (1962), Sussman (1965) and Adams (1970) provide useful reviews on American research.
2 For example, Hodges and Smith (1954); Lupton and Mitchell (1954); Dennis, Henriques and Slaughter (1956); Mogey (1956); Seeley, Sim and Loosley (1956); Williams (1956); Frankenberg (1957); Stacey (1960); Tunstall (1962); Littlejohn (1963); Gans (1967); Hollowell (1968); Goldthorpe et al. (1969); Pahl and Pahl (1971); Oxley (1974); Salaman (1974); Hill (1976).
3 Many American community studies have been more concerned with status group formation, joint voluntary association membership, and the effects of propinquity than with the nature of different types of personal relationship, e.g. Warner and Lunt devote fifty pages of their chapter on 'The formal and informal associations of Yankee City' to formal associations and only five (of which two and a half are taken up with tables and diagrams) to informal association.

Chapter 2

Ways of Seeing

In this chapter I shall consider one of the core problems in studying patterns of sociability: the problem of how to analyse individual sociable relationships. The term 'pattern of sociability' here simply refers to the composite organisation of those sociable relationships that the individual sustains in his social life. It consists of nothing more than the sum of all these individual relationships. Given this, it follows that a satisfactory analysis of patterns of sociability depends on a previous adequate analysis of the sociable relationships of which they are comprised. The question to be answered in this chapter, then, is: how can such an analysis of sociable relationships be achieved?

It is paradoxical that this question needs asking, for a good deal of research in sociology has been concerned, in part at least, with analysing sociable relationships of one sort or another. Kinship studies, occupational studies, community studies, and many others, all concern themselves at times with describing and analysing these relationships. If they have all managed, why is it necessary here to discuss at length how such an analysis can be achieved? Why not just follow the lead they have given?

One reason for specifying the way relationships are to be analysed is that this is rarely done in the literature. The theoretical framework that analysts impose upon sociable relationships is usually not examined critically; it remains implicit in their work rather than being made explicit. The reasons for this are not hard to find. To begin with, although sociable relationships are highly complex phenomena with many facets to them, a great number of studies concern themselves with only very limited aspects of relationships. How to measure the aspect of the relationship with which they are concerned is often self-evident and straightforward. Thus, for example, if one is interested in the social isolation of a group of people it can be argued that all one needs to know about their relationships is the amount of interaction they entail. Although this may seem a narrow way of studying social isolation it does at least have the advantage of being straightforward and clear-cut. The same applies to other specific aspects of relationships that can be readily conceptualised in a manner that makes measurement simple. A further reason why some studies do not discuss the theoretical framework they use in analysing sociable relationships is that their concern with these relationships is only a small, relatively minor part of their overall study. They are not important enough to the design of the study to warrant a detailed theoretical account. Sociable relationships can be dealt with in a straightforward common-sense way, without the need for any questioning of how their portrayal is being achieved. This is the case, for example, in most occupational and community studies.

The present study, however, is directly concerned with sociable relationships; and its focus is on their overall content, which I take to include the meanings and definitions that the actors themselves place on them as well as more readily apparent aspects of them. In other words, what is to be analysed in this study is the nature of the involvement of an individual with a variety of others. Now, terms like 'nature of the involvement', 'content', 'definitions' and 'meanings' are both complex and imprecise; they may be taken as implying a number of different things. Certainly they cannot be operationalised in as obvious a way as can 'amount of interaction' or 'frequency of contact'. Hence the need for an explicit account of the theoretical framework that is to be used.

SOCIOLOGICAL PERSPECTIVES OF SOCIABLE RELATIONSHIPS

Without a doubt the dominant techniques used for measuring sociable relationships in most empirical research depend upon contact rates: how often a person is seen or communicated with. It is important to note that in many studies contact rates are used not only to measure the amount of interaction, but also as an indicator of the *quality* of a relationship. Now, intuitively this does not seem to be unreasonable. If one person is seen quite regularly and another hardly at all, then, other factors being equal – for example, the distance and expense involved, the health and physical mobility of the interactants, and so on – it is quite sensible to assume that the individual concerned has a fuller and more significant relationship with the former than the latter. Alone, though, contact rates do not provide a basis for differentiating between the content and nature of different relationships. They cannot indicate what is involved in a relationship, what form it takes, or what meaning those party to it bestow upon it. While many studies also include case histories and other detailed illustrations of the sort of services and exchanges that take place in a typical relationship, when hard 'scientific' measures are required so that comparisons of people's relationships can be made, contact rates reign supreme. In particular, this is true of kinship studies, and most noticeably of the earlier ones.

This reliance on 'contact' is both reasonable and justified in so far as many of the problems these authors concerned themselves with require such basic information. It is less justified, though, in analyses of the type of solidarity embodied in relationships. Once a putative relationship has been shown to be 'active', other measures and ways of analysing it are necessary.

While something of a fetish undoubtedly exists about the use of quantitative measures of interaction in kinship studies, not all researchers have relied on them to the same extent in analysing sociable relationships. At the risk of oversimplifying, the content of relationships has been analysed from two other major perspectives: (1) as systems of exchange; and (2) in terms of their emotional and affectional qualities. To take the latter point first, many community and kinship studies communicate the character of relationships by referring to their affective properties. To some – in Barker's words, those 'socialised to an "affective" view of the family' (1972, p. 586) – such a way of looking at relationships may seem especially suitable in kinship studies. Frequently there is a form of 'social distance' scale implied in such measures, though only Firth, Hubert and Forge state explicitly the categories they use in analysing the emotional/affectional quality of personal relationships. Comments like: 'The old man's not so bad . . . but I don't get on with (the wife's) mother . . . She's always going on about something' (Young and Willmott, 1962, p. 66), 'You must talk to the neighbours but you mustn't say too much', 'I keep myself to myself, I do' (Mogey, 1956, pp. 83 and 84) and 'I never really liked my brother John . . . We just weren't very good at living with each other' (Firth *et al.*, 1970, p. 435) reflect the level of generality typical of this approach, though it needs to be remembered that no study relies on it alone.

Far more important than social distance measures of affection is a concern with the exchange and transactional basis of relationships. Formal exchange theory plays little part in most studies – Barker's study (1972) of young people's relations with their parents is one of the few investigations to use an explicit exchange model for analysing relationships – but many, in considering the functions of various categories of other, are concerned with the services individuals exchange with one another. Well-known examples are the kinship studies by Young and Willmott (1962) and Bell (1968*b*). In a similar way a number of network studies are also concerned with exchange or 'transactional' content in relationships. Of the empirical studies Kapferer's (1969) is the most complete, though even his five types – conversation; joking behaviour; job assistance; personal service; and cash assistance – are too broad to differentiate between essentially similar relationships as is required in the present text.

This, indeed, is the major difficulty with this perspective in general: the categories involved tend to be rather imprecise. To a degree, this is because a 'function' rather than an explicit 'exchange' model predominates, with researchers being satisfied to point out the functions that different categories of people perform for each other. For the present purpose categories like 'giving affection', 'being a leisure companion' or 'providing support' are too broad to be helpful; yet it is difficult to be more precise within these 'functional' terms. They are useful where there is a wide range in the type of function performed, but less so where there is a basic similarity.

RULES OF RELEVANCE

Having discussed the models used in previous empirical research for understanding social relationships, I want now to develop the framework to be used in this study. The concern is with understanding the character of the solidarity involved in different relationships in a manner that allows comparisons to be made between them. Because the solidarity evinced in any relationship is a consequence of the way it is structured by those party to it, the framework adopted must pay heed to people's subjective definitions of their relationships as well as the more usual objective measures of interaction. The sociological stance most compatible with these aims is symbolic interactionism. More than other perspectives, a symbolic interactionist one emphasises the importance of the individual's understanding of the social world he experiences, and his own part in creating and structuring it. Throughout the analysis that follows the influence of symbolic interactionist thought will be evident. More specifically, the framework I have adopted here is derived from a theoretical paper on friendship by Robert Paine entitled 'In search of friendship' (1969). In this paper Paine is concerned with raising the questions that need answering if friendship is to be placed 'within the realm of the phenomenologically larger order of things to which it belongs . . . [the realm] of interpersonal relations as a whole' (p. 506). Above all else, Paine desires to point to the differences between friendships and other forms of personal relationships, and to illustrate the structural features of a society that allows friendships to be formed. He emphasises the private and personal nature of friendship in our society, suggesting that these are its distinguishing features.

However, the section of his paper most relevant here is that in which, following Barth (1966), he discusses 'two universal diacritica of interpersonal relationships for which generative primacy may be claimed' (1969, p. 509). Paine is interested in the range of behaviour that can be tolerated in any type of relationship and suggests using the limits of this range as a basis for comparing types. That is, he is concerned with the 'boundaries' of relationships: with 'the delineation of social relationships in terms of the bounds of their permitted content and conduct' (1969, p. 509). He recognises that structural anthropologists, with their notions of set constraints, rights and duties, have viewed relationships too rigidly, and wants to incorporate into this approach that of Goffman and his followers who see relationships as strategically based with (potentially) ever-changing rights and advantages. Thus Paine desires to look at variation in relationships by creating a model that fuses the effects of corporate structure and contextual 'infra-structure' on relationships. To do this he introduces the concepts 'rules of relevancy' and 'standards of equivalency'.

The first of these, the rules of relevancy of relationships, is the more intriguing, and is offered as 'a necessary mediating notion between the "by charter" and "by strategy" . . . views of the bounds of human relationships' (1969, p. 510). The rules of relevancy determine what is pertinent to a relationship, what is permissible and desirable and what is 'out of bounds'. The more the relationship is based in the corporate structure, the more rigid and inflexible the rules of relevancy are; conversely the more a relationship is founded on contextual elements and the 'strategic disposition' of those involved, the more flexible they will be.

Paine does not develop the idea of 'rules of relevancy' at any length; nor does he that of 'standards of equivalency', apart from noting that all relationships are based on exchange between the parties: 'the nature of the exchanges varies and its description, in each case, tells one much about the nature of the relationship' (1969, p. 511). Here Paine is basically reformulating Simmel's point that all interaction is a system of on-going exchange. Overall there seems no reason why 'standards of equivalency' cannot be incorporated and subsumed into a slightly broadened notion of 'rules of relevancy', because, as Paine points out, any particular type of relationship is defined to a large part by the sort of exchange that is relevant to it. Further, the idea of rules of relevancy (or rules of relevance, as I prefer to term them), can be applied to individual relationships as well as to generic types (e.g. 'friend', 'patron', 'client'), the latter being the level at which Paine discusses them. The concept can as easily be used to conceptualise the differences in one's relationships with, say, an uncle and an employer. The remainder of this chapter develops the idea of rules of relevance along these lines.

The first point to make clear is that, in claiming that rules of relevance exist which govern the content of relationships, I am not suggesting (and nor, I think, is Paine), that people explicitly formulate these rules and then construct their relationship around them. Unlike commercial, professional or business relationships, there are no charters or constitutions for regulating the sociable relationships between friends and acquaintances, or even those between adult kin (apart from the spouse relationship). Rather, the rules of relevance to which I am referring are implicit in these relationships; they are not deliberated on or carefully worked out, but develop in the course of interaction. They serve not to protect the interests of those concerned, but to bound and structure relationships so that interaction can be achieved unproblematically.

This can be put another way. Any relationship comprises a series of interactions, each interaction between those involved being but one part or episode of the relationship. These episodic interactions are not random and unformed; they are not single isolated events unrelated to one another. Rather they constitute a series in more than the temporal sense, for what goes on in prior interactions forms, influences and inhibits – in a word, *structures* – what goes on in later ones. There is, generally, a 'thread' linking interactions that allows the interactants (and outsiders for that matter) to conceive of them as episodes in an on-going unitary relationship. If this were not so, relationships could never develop beyond an elementary level, an evidently absurd proposition. Indexicality plays its part, so that in the course of the series of interactions the interactants come implicitly to define the boundaries of the relationship and decide on what is relevant and appropriate to it. In the process they structure the path future episodes of interaction will follow. Naturally the rules of relevance applied in any given relationship are likely to change as the situation of the interactants changes. They are not fixed and given, as few relationships remain static. Instead the rules of relevance applied develop and evolve over the course of the interaction. Nevertheless, at any given time the interactants have some definition of their relationship and some notion of what is and is not relevant to it.

Thus relationships do not exist in cognitive vacuums; they are ordered by the participants to a greater or lesser extent. If this were not so, it would be impossible to carry on the relationships satisfactorily for they would lack form and structure. To claim that all relationships need to be structured and limited if they are to make sense to those involved does not mean that relationships exist only at an 'ideal' level. Quite obviously they are manifested at a behavioural level, and the behaviour of the interactants can be used to check the consistency of the reported definitions the interactants hold of their relationship. If the notion of rules of relevance is to prove useful in the sociological analysis of relationships, then there must be a high correlation between the 'ideal' and the behavioural. Indeed, this is built into the model to the extent that those in the relationship can 'do' the relationship. Their ability to bring off the relationship empirically is equated with their ability to understand to their own satisfaction what they are doing. (Of course this does not necessarily mean that they can make the implicit explicit, and communicate to an outside party the basis of any relationship. This is an entirely separate matter.)

These implicit cognitive mappings that those party to a relationship have about their involvement in it are what I mean by the rules of relevance. Given that at any particular time the interaction between the parties in a relationship depends to a great extent on the way they define it and on what they see as relevant to it, then what they do define as relevant can be used to delineate that relationship. That is, the principles or rules that are used implicitly by the interactants in ordering a relationship, and which serve them as a basis for knowing how to act in, and what to expect of, a relationship, can also, once they are abstracted and made explicit, be used for analysing and comparing different relationships.

While I have termed these cognitive mappings 'rules' of relevance, they clearly differ from more formal rules in that they are nowhere recorded or written down. Instead they are implicit in social action most of the time. Provided the relationship is found worthwhile and satisfactory to all the parties, there is normally no need for reflection about the implicit rules of relevance that govern it. In general, it is probably only when there is a unilateral 'breaking' of the rules that the rules themselves are ever likely to be brought into the open and made explicit. In other words, it is normally only in default that the rules are ever likely to become a topic of discussion. One common example of this is when one party in what has previously been a platonic male–female relationship desires to change the relationship's rules of relevance by bringing a sexual element into play. If the other party does not wish to change the relationship in this way, he or she is likely to either opt out of it altogether or gently make explicit the relationship's asexual basis. Though simple, such an example, which in one form or another has probably been experienced by most people, illustrates how implicit rules of relevance may be made explicit when the relationship's basis is threatened. While generally more subtle, the same mechanism applies to other areas apart from the sexual, and to other sorts of relationships. Of course if both sides wish the basis of their relationship to change, or at least are not against it doing so, then this can occur gradually without the previous rules ever being made explicit. The development of relationships can be seen as the ebb and flow of rules of relevance and the gradual change of what they cover.

From the above, it is evident that the rules of relevance of a relationship are akin to what are normally known in the sociological literature as 'roles'. These, too, are thought of as cognitive abstractions used by people for ordering their expectations about what is involved in a particular social setting. They, too, are taken to provide a framework for knowing what is appropriate and relevant in a given situation, and what is not. So why not use a form of role analysis rather than a new concept like rules of relevance? One difficulty with the concept of roles is the confusion there is over what they are exactly. The concept has been interpreted in a variety of ways. There is little in common, for example, between Linton's structuralist and essentially deterministic views and Ralph Turner's more free-ranging, interactionist ones. The concept of rules of relevance side-steps this confusion. A more important reason for using rules of relevance is that generally roles are taken as an abstraction of what the 'average' or 'normal' performer of a status position can be expected to do. They are thus much broader and less specific than rules of relevance as used here. Consequently an analysis of behaviour in terms of roles tends to neglect differences that exist in the way people behave in order to generalise about those things that are common to the performances of a given status. The aim here is not only to see what all brothers or all mates have in common in their relationships with one another but also to analyse the variants that are found empirically in the way these positions are acted out. Rules of relevance allow abstraction from each relationship, rather than being generalised models.

Nevertheless, the two concepts are related, especially when role is viewed from a symbolic interactionist rather than a structuralist perspective. For example, one way of understanding the concept of role is to see it as equivalent to the rules of relevance applied by someone involved in a typical relationship. In other words, the role 'friend' can be seen as consisting simply of the rules of relevance adopted by a person in what is taken as a typical 'friend' relationship. For such purpose it matters little that such a typical relationship may not exist empirically. Another way the concepts are related is through the actor's idea of what is involved in a role influencing the rules of relevance that emerge in his relationships with others. Each of us, whether he is a sociologist or not, carries around with him some more or less vague idea of what is expected of, say, a friend; that is, he has some notion of the role of 'friend'. When we become friends with someone, this vague notion, while by no means determining the way we behave, does provide a back-cloth of knowledge of what is appropriate. The rules of relevance of any particular relationship can be seen as being constructed against this backcloth. The latter influences and bounds the way the former develop. However, despite these similarities, the concept of 'rules of relevance' seems of greater utility for the present purposes than the idea of 'role' as normally used because it allows the basis of individual relationships to be analysed more readily.

An important problem that remains is how the rules of relevance of a relationship are to be analysed. Given that they are largely tacit in most relationships and have consequently to be made explicit, the analyst needs to have some notion of what areas he is going to concentrate on in drawing them out. He must know where and for what to look. One aspect of relationships that is of concern here is the *range* of social settings and activities in which individuals meet with particular others. While there is a very wide variety of situations in which it is possible to see another person, in practice the settings for interaction in any relationship are restricted. Generally a relationship is defined and constructed in such a way that meetings only take place in certain types of setting, with interaction in other sorts of situation being seen as inappropriate. It is this property of relationships that can be used initially for analysing rules of relevance. It has elements in common with social distance measures in that, like them, it is concerned with what people feel able to do together, though unlike the more formal of these it does not assume ordinal scaling of activities.

Interest here is not solely with the social settings and activities in which meetings most commonly occur. The concept of rules of relevance is somewhat wider than this and denotes the way the relationship is cognitively structured by the participants. The whole range of situations in which the participants consider it appropriate to meet each other must be analysed, and not only those one or two in which they happen to see one another most. If they define their relationship as relevant only to one setting, then clearly they will only organise interaction in that setting. But it does not necessarily follow that because two people usually meet in one particular setting they define their relationship as limited only to that setting. They may conceive of their relationship in a wider way, and recognise that, while in fact it is not, it could be activated in a number of other settings quite readily. This conception of rules of relevance brings us to more precarious ground, or at least highlights an inherent difficulty as it means deciding on the veracity and consistency of people's accounts of their behaviour in, and attitudes towards, their sociable relationships. These difficulties are inevitable in some form and must be faced in order to understand the way a respondent defines his relationships and the meaning they have for him. Clearly in all cases the actual settings and activities in which a relationship in fact takes place are the most important features in analysing this aspect of the rules of relevance of a relationship. All I am claiming is that care must be taken that a relationship is not thought of as defined as limited to a particular setting simply because interaction happens to occur most commonly in that setting.

In summary, this chapter has argued that previous studies' dependence on quantitative measures of relationships is somewhat narrow and limited. Where the aim is to contrast the character of the solidarity implicit in relationships, the meaning they have for the interactants must be considered as well. The argument here is that relationships do not occur haphazardly but rather are constructed and shaped by those involved according to principles which are consequent on the definitions they hold of their relationships. Therefore, in order to understand the solidarity embedded in relationships, a framework needs to be created that incorporates their subjective as well as their objective features. Such a framework is provided by the concept of rules of relevance. This formulation has the advantage that it focuses upon both the regular patterning behind relationships and the part played by the interactants in their construction and maintenance. It is this duality that makes the concept useful for analysing the solidarity present in different types of relationship.

Chapter 3

The Selden Hey Study

As noted in Chapter 1, many of the themes to be raised in the chapters that follow will be illustrated with material taken from a study of patterns of sociability that the author conducted in the early 1970s (see Allan, 1976). In order that the reader may have some basis for evaluating these examples, this chapter will be concerned with describing the fieldwork procedures used in that study. These were based on the 'depth' or 'focused' interview. The alternative way of gathering data on 'sociability networks' (Edgell, n.d.) or 'first order stars' (Barnes, 1969) is to use observational and self-report techniques. This method was rejected because it inevitably limits the sample to one or two individuals (see Boswell, 1966; Epstein, 1969) and thus makes comparison of the ways in which different people order their set of sociable relationships difficult. Furthermore, there is general agreement amongst sociologists who have attempted to study sets of personal relationships in our own society that it is in many cases inappropriate to do so by methods mainly dependent on observation. The content of many personal relationships is considered private in our society and many tend to take place, either literally or metaphorically, behind closed doors, as Frankenberg appreciated in his hillside lament (Frankenberg, 1969, p. 16).

For these reasons the depth interview was judged more appropriate than observational techniques, even though the former is not as reliable because it depends more on the respondent's memory. The advantage of unstructured, informal interviews is that, more than most other forms of data collection, they allow for the respondent's subjective interpretation of his relationships, as well as more objective facts about them, to be made evident. This is most suitable for the present purposes as it is consonant with the way that the concept of rules of relevance has been formulated above. The method also allows a relatively large number of relationships to be compared. It is possible to contrast what the actor sees as relevant to one with what he sees as relevant to another. In this way a more complete picture of both can emerge.

THE RESEARCH SETTING

The research took place in a small commuter village in East Anglia that I shall call Selden Hey. Before the empirical research started in earnest, the feasibility of the techniques to be used for collecting data on respondents' sociability stars (i.e. the total set of sociable relationships they maintain with others, see Barnes, 1969) was checked by trying them out, either in full or in part, on a small number of pre-sample respondents. By chance, one of the families interviewed at this stage lived in Selden Hey, and contact with the village then suggested it would be a suitable place to carry out the research proper, for while it is small it is also heterogeneous. It seemed that it would be possible to find as much variation in style of life, and hence star construction, here as it would be anywhere, given that the overall size of the sample was to be small by conventional standards. Largely this is because of its geographical position. There are three large towns within a radius of 10 miles of the village, which provide a range of employment and service facilities. In addition the village is within 2 miles of the main Norwich to London road, and the inter-city railway line connecting the towns of East Anglia to London passes through the village. Consequently there is a regular and swift passenger service to London from the village.

Selden Hey is, by common consent, an attractive village. Some of its buildings are of historic interest, and its setting is complemented by the small stream that runs down the north side of the village and the expanse of common, protected by Royal Charter, that forms its centre-piece. At one time, as well as providing grazing for the village animals, the common was used for annual fairs, horse races and lamb sales. Now its use is restricted to the play of children, the exercise of dogs and the sporting efforts of the local football and cricket teams, but the villagers in general remain proud of it, and newcomers especially think it represents much of what English village life is, or rather was, all about.

Until the Second World War, Selden Hey was an agricultural village and small market centre. Since then its character has changed quite radically. Although there are still some farms within it, the village is now a dormitory for the surrounding towns and, increasingly, for London. In the 1950s a large council estate was built, as were many individual private homes for people willing to commute to work each day to the nearby towns. The most significant change in the population structure occurred in the 1960s, with the building of a large new private housing estate. Within a period of seven years nearly 250 new houses were built, which resulted in an increase in the population of the village of over 40 per cent (from slightly under 1,400 to slightly over 2,000). This rapid expansion has by no means met with the full approval of all the 'old villagers', as some feel that the building of the estate has spoilt the charm of their village. Certainly the increase in population has had its effects. While local businesses, clubs and societies are prospering, the village's elementary school is having some difficulty with overcrowding as the vast majority of the occupants of the new houses are couples with young children.

Although I have no accurate figures on this, my impression is that most of the people who have moved into the houses on the estate do not come from the immediate area of Selden Hey, but have moved there either because the price of housing has forced them out of London and its hinterland, or because they have obtained work in one of the neighbouring towns. The majority of those employed appear to work within 10 miles of Selden Hey, though very few within the village itself, while a substantial minority of both men and women commute daily to London to work. The train journey to the capital takes little more than double the half-hour needed to drive into the neighbouring towns in the morning rush hour.

SELECTION OF THE SAMPLE

As suggested above, it was apparent from the beginning that intensive, 'in-depth' interviewing was necessary. Respondents would have to be interviewed a number of times if a reasonably full sociability star was to be obtained from each of them, and if each relationship in that star was to be discussed individually. Inevitably this meant that the total number of respondents that could be interviewed was limited. A total sample of about fifty people seemed a reasonable one for which to aim. That number would allow at least a limited range of different types of sociability star to be collected, yet remain manageable for an individual researcher.

Although the sample was to be so small, it was considered important to ensure that its selection was such that both middle- and working-class male and female respondents were included. All previous research on patterns of sociability had pointed to the importance of these structural variables, especially that of class. Taking a random sample seemed the least satisfactory way of obtaining respondents, as its main advantage, that of making certain that there had been an unbiased selection of respondents and, therefore, supposedly ensuring that as wide as possible a variety of life-styles was included, would be invalidated by the small size of the sample. Further, together with other statistically based sampling techniques, it would be as effective a method as one could find for ignoring any circumstances that might help in the collection and analysis of stars.

A more appropriate solution appeared to be the selection of a sample on the basis of neighbourhood groupings: that is, by asking the occupants of blocks of adjacent houses to co-operate in the study. By selecting diverse blocks, each block containing similar houses, the problem of obtaining respondents from different socio-economic groups could be overcome. While there were no lists available which gave information about individuals' 'class position' there is a pronounced tendency in our society for people in a similar economic situation to have houses together, and to be separated from those whose economic position is different. This *de facto* stratification, brought about by the economic structure of housing in this country, provides a simple, yet reasonably effective, way of ensuring that respondents from the two major socio-economic groups are included in a small sample.

Further, basing the sample on people living in adjacent housing raised the possibility that some useful information might be obtained through general gossip. More important, it meant that the respondents were able to discuss the research (and the researcher) with one another, and hopefully thereby increase their perception of the importance of their co-operation in it.

It was also decided that interviewing both husbands and wives was warranted as married couples often interact sociably with others as a couple. Some of the people who are part of an individual's sociability star are also likely to be part of his or her spouse's star. The proportion of the stars that are joint will vary from couple to couple, as Bott's work indicates, but in any case with most couples each side has some knowledge of the people with whom his or her spouse interacts. It seemed better to use this knowledge than ignore it. The pre-sample interviews had suggested that couples would probably be able to assist each other in recalling the various people each knew, thereby making the recorded stars fuller than they would have been if only one of the couple had been interviewed. Consequently, instead of basing the sample on selected individuals, wherever possible husbands and wives were interviewed. This policy also served to ensure that the number of stars collected from one sex would be approximately equal to the number collected from the other.

Three diverse blocks of adjacent houses were chosen, one from the new housing estate, one from the council estate and the third from a road containing older, individually styled, privately owned houses. Together they were representative of much of the housing in Selden Hey. Occupants of twenty-three of the twenty-nine houses in the three selected blocks agreed to be interviewed: eight in the private estate block; eight in the council estate block; and seven in the other private block. In eighteen of the twenty-three houses both husband and wife were interviewed; in a further three the wife alone was interviewed as their husbands were 'too busy' or 'not really interested in this sort of thing'. The remaining two houses were occupied by single people. This meant that in all forty-one respondents were interviewed. Tables 3.1 to 3.4 provide demographic and other information about these forty-one respondents. In Table 3.1, and throughout this book, class is defined by occupation. Where the male was in non-manual employment his household was classified as middle class, and where he was employed in manual work his household was classified as working class. (For a fuller discussion of this issue, see the Appendix.)

Table 3.1   *Social Class and Sex of the Respondents*

	Male	Female
Middle-class	10	11
Working-class	9	11

Table 3.2   *Age at Time of Research*

Age	Number of respondents
20–29	13
30–39	8
40–49	8
50–59	6
60 or Over	6

Table 3.3   *Family Cycle Position*

State	Number of respondents
Unmarried	1
Married without children	12
Married with non-dependent children	10
Married with dependent children	17
Widowed	1

Table 3.4   *Household Composition*

Composition	Number of respondents
Alone	1
With spouse only	16
With spouse and children	21
With other kin	3

There is no way of knowing if the sample used in this research is representative of some wider universe. Its size and the manner in which it was constructed mean that there can be no grounds for adducing whether it is or not. Consequently generalisations made from the study need to be interpreted cautiously. On the other hand there is little *a priori* reason to suppose that the sample is an exceptionally biased one. The range of Tables 3.1 to 3.4 makes it reasonable to assume that some of the differences that there may be between the ways that individual relationships, and therefore stars, are commonly constructed by different groups of people will be covered.

STAR CONSTRUCTION

The concept of 'star' in the sense used here is totally foreign to most people: they can go about their everyday life interacting with those they know without ever having any need to collate those people. A similar difficulty has been experienced by researchers studying kin relationships (see Barnes, 1967) but on a somewhat reduced scale as the idea of a genealogy is well known in our culture. Certainly, the construction of genealogies by interview methods is far easier than the construction of stars by these methods, for genealogies are based on a logical system which is used by respondents to structure their social world while stars are not. Genealogies involve a series of operations which people continually use naturally without the sociologist's demand. The researcher interested in kinship is able to use this structuring as a means of data collection precisely because it provides a logical framework, understood by both researcher and respondent, by means of which all those who are recognised as kin can be systematically detailed. Further, because the elementary family is the unit around which people commonly order their thoughts on kinship, separating kin as a whole into these smaller entities facilitates respondents' recall, and makes the data collection process simpler and more meaningful for them. Consequently it becomes more reliable too.

Unfortunately sociability stars cannot be collected in such a systematic way as these factors do not apply with them. There is no model that can be used which systematically covers all those who might be included. It is impossible to start with 'ego' and work one's way out through his star by relating each new person to someone already noted, as there is no necessary connection between the various people involved. Further, there are only limited and incomplete ways in which a star can be split into smaller units, comparable to elementary families, which can be used to 'jog' the memory and facilitate recall through being units in terms of which people normally organise their experiences.

Stars therefore have to be collected in a much more idiosyncratic manner, for the character of each star depends upon the activities of the central 'ego'. Finding out what these activities are, what the person does with his life, what opportunities he has to meet and interact with others, is one of the essential tasks of constructing stars. By isolating each area of activity, an individual's sociable relationships can be separated into categories according to the particular circumstance that led to the relationship being formed (e.g. kin, workmates, neighbours, fellow club, church or lodge members, etc.). While most of these categories lack any internal structure that allows us systematically to collect all those who are involved in them, they at least allow the mass of relationships to be divided into smaller units which enable a respondent to remember the individuals in them with greater ease.

Not everyone who is known to a respondent will necessarily be uncovered by these techniques, but at least they provide a partially systematic framework which helps respondents to recollect and name the various people they know. Clearly they will be more successful the more routine a person's life, and the narrower his range of activities, for the more varied and changing a person's life is, the less he will be able to separate into definite categories the activities and situations in which he is involved. In addition, there are often other sources available to check that major figures in a respondent's life have not been omitted. These sources are the documents that many respondents keep for various purposes which either list or make reference to a number of their (more important) associates. Telephone lists, address books and Christmas card lists are the most obvious, but diaries, wedding and party lists may prove useful as well. By combining these approaches and carefully following all the leads offered by a respondent, it is possible to construct a comparatively full star even though it can never be done as systematically or as confidently as a genealogy.

One difficulty with star construction is knowing when to stop the process. The researcher has to decide what to do with people whom a respondent knows but does not know at all well. For example, there are the people a respondent sees in the pub but only says 'hello' to; people he passes in the neighbourhood and nods at; or people at work he only chats to on the few occasions he happens to end up behind them in the dinner queue. In the end it would seem that each researcher must make his own decision, consistent with the broad objectives of his study, about the sort of interaction that is necessary for a person to qualify for a place in a respondent's sociability star.

It is here that a problem arises between those categories of relationship that have some form of internal structuring (e.g. neighbours, but especially kin), and those which do not. There is a danger of collecting too few of the latter but too many of the former. Thus, for example, it is not unlikely that a respondent's presented genealogy will include people the respondent has never met, or met at most only once or twice in his life. Although such people are part of his kin, in what sense are they part of his star? Because of such factors there may be an imbalance between the information gathered about different categories of relationship. It is important, then, to remember in the analysis possible divergencies in the information obtained about the full range of people known in the different categories, and certainly there is no case for making any comparison of the numbers of each category involved in a person's star, at least not without considering the effects of the way the numbers were obtained.

THE INTERVIEWS

All the interviews took place in the respondents' homes, usually in the evening, though occasionally, where it suited a respondent better, in the morning or afternoon. Where both a husband and wife had agreed to take part, they were generally interviewed together, although again this also varied depending on the respondents' availability, However, as interviews were arranged beforehand, it was usually possible to find an occasion when both wife and husband could be present. The modal number of interviews for each 'home' was four, though here too there was some variation. The length of each interview varied from between three-quarters of an hour to over three and a half hours, with ninety minutes to two hours being the usual length. This meant respondents were seen for between five and eight hours in total.

The general aim of the research was to get the respondents to discuss freely their sociable relationships. It was to be expected that most respondents would experience some difficulty in doing this, for many of the relationships they were being asked to discuss are traditionally thought of as private and of concern only to those involved in them. There was a tendency for the interviews to be more formal, in the sense that they consisted of answers given to specific questions, at the beginning of the series of interviews than at the end. Only as the respondents became more familiar with the research and the interview situation were they able to relax and discuss their sociable relationships fully. The situation in which the interviews take place can help in this process. Most of the interviews took place in the living-room or lounge with both the respondents and myself sitting in easy chairs. This helped in its small way in creating the necessary definition of the research aims. In the few cases where I was sat at a kitchen or dining-room table ('Then you'll have something to write on'), the situation came to be defined more as a question-and-answer session than one in which the respondents talked around their sociable relationships. Where the interviews took place in the less formal setting of the lounge or living-room, a less formal definition of the situation prevailed, with conversation flowing more freely.

The decision to interview husbands and wives jointly was taken partly because of the difficulty of interviewing people separately from their spouses in their own home, but mainly because, as many couples interact sociably as a unit, together they are able to create a fuller picture of each of their sociability stars than either would alone. On the other hand, some couples lead more segregated sociable lives. If they have carefully ensured that their spouse knows little of what they do or whom they see, they are not going to destroy this for the sake of giving a stranger an accurate account. In such cases, the account a person gives in front of his (or her) spouse of his (or her) sociable relationships is bound to be suspect. However, the evidence available suggests that few couples lead as private and segregated sociable lives as this. Through living together, each side almost inevitably possesses a great deal of valid knowledge of the other's activities. Nevertheless, the dangers of getting biased or invalid data through making the interview situation a joint one have to be recognised.

On the other hand, there are positive benefits accruing from joint interviews, benefits which are not often recognised. As well as the advantages already mentioned, an unexpected feature was the extent to which respondents modified the account of a relationship given by their spouse. What frequently occurred, especially in later interviews, was that I would ask one side about a relationship and get an account of it from him or her, but all the while receive cues from the other that suggested that this was not the way it really was. While his or her view of the way a relationship 'really' was was not necessarily more valid than the original account, this implicit and explicit questioning of it often resulted in the two of them setting up a dialogue about the relationship which gave me a great deal of useful information (see Allan, in press).

As mentioned above, most respondents were interviewed four times. The first interview consisted of collecting genealogies, obtaining information about the age, occupation and residence of the people included in it, and discussing the sociable relationships the respondents had with these people. While by anthropological standards one ninety-minute interview is not a great deal of time in which to collect two genealogies, it sufficed here as the main concern was with collecting details of those kin who were significant members of the respondents' stars. Data on kinship were collected first because, being structured, they are the easiest to gather. It thus served as a satisfactory way of introducing respondents to the interview situation and to the type of information in which I was interested.

In the second interview I tried to get the same information

for non-kin members of the respondents' stars. For the reasons discussed earlier in this chapter, this is a far harder task than obtaining information on kin. Often the third and fourth interviews were partly spent adding to these data. At first the task was also hampered somewhat by the terminology used in asking the questions. I tended at the beginning to start the interviews by saying: 'Last time we talked about your relatives. This time I want to do the same sort of thing with your friends.' The respondents were then asked about their friends at a particular stage in their life, and from this beginning the inquiry was expanded to include all the various situations in which they met others sociably. However this format tended to place too much emphasis on those the respondents labelled 'friends' at the expense of 'non-friends' whom they knew. The reasons for not asking specifically about friends are obvious in retrospect – mainly that the concept 'friend' is variable, depending as it does on an ill-defined subjective evaluation of a relationship rather than on an objective, readily ascertained feature of structure external to the relationship – but they were not at the time. It was only after conducting a number of interviews in this way that I realised that I was demanding an implicit evaluation from my respondents, and that, because of this evaluation, the stars I was collecting were likely to be more limited than they need be. This bias was rectified in later interviews when the respondents were asked more definitely about those others they knew but did not regard as 'friends'. On the other hand, the fact that the concept 'friend' demands an evaluation means that it is a useful starting point around which to base a discussion of the various relationships that a person has.

The third and fourth interviews were spent mainly discussing these relationships, trying to get the respondent to talk about them and compare them. By then the respondents were more used to the interview situation and research process. The discussion was based on such questions as the occasions on which they met, the types of activity in which they engaged, the kinds of topics they discussed, what they considered 'private' from these people or at least not of their concern, the services and help they exchanged with each other, and so on. In these interviews the respondents were also asked to detail those people they had seen sociably in the previous month, and to describe again their typical sociable habits and activities. Any reference to individuals or areas of activity that had not been mentioned before were raised and discussed in full. In this way the star membership that was recorded was expanded and checked throughout all the interviews.

The fieldwork ended when the main data necessary for analysing the central issues of the research had been collected. At this stage some of the respondents were also beginning to tire of the exercise.

On the fourth and fifth visits one or two respondents said things like 'Good heavens! Are you back again? I thought we'd told you everything you wanted to know.' or 'How many more visits are there going to be, then?' Not all the respondents felt like this about the research, one husband going so far as to say, jokingly: 'We're going to miss you when you stop coming. You give us something to talk about!' Nevertheless, the point remains that the researcher must be considerate of his respondents and not exploit their co-operation too greatly. Elizabeth Bott has remarked that it is inappropriate to knock on people's doors and ask them to undergo intensive interviews (Bott, 1971, p. 12). Instead the researcher should try to obtain volunteers, people who appreciate the inconvenience the research will cause but who are none the less willing to take part. Certainly this would seem to be so if the research calls for respondents being interviewed more than four or five times. Below this number most people will co-operate fairly readily, but above it whatever satisfaction taking part provides is increasingly overcome by the tediousness of answering questions on what, no doubt, seem to many to be irrelevant and uninteresting questions. Only those who are most fascinated by the study and who have built up a particularly strong relationship with the researcher will be willing to continue co-operating with the research in the same spirit.

Chapter 4

The Nature of
Friendship and Kinship

Both kinship and friendship are socially bestowed. That is, the labels of kinship and friendship are only applied to others who satisfy certain social criteria. It is the task of this chapter to specify what those criteria are. A major theme will be that the criteria of friendship are of a different order from those of kinship, in that the former involves an evaluation of a continuing social relationship while the latter depends largely on factors external to the character of on-going interaction. Because kinship as a cultural construct has been analysed so fully elsewhere (cf. Firth, 1956; Williams, 1963; Schneider, 1968, 1969, 1972; Firth *et al.*, 1970; Schneider and Smith, 1973), I shall concentrate far more in this chapter on the properties of friendship. This is necessary because, as Paine notes, anthropological discussions of friendship 'are notable for beginning and ending with, let us say, tribal bond-friendship or the Mesoamerican bond of *compadrazgo*' (1969, p. 509).

ASPECTS OF KINSHIP IN WESTERN CULTURE

In the previous chapter I suggested that finding out who a person's kin are is far easier than finding out who his friends are, for kinship is structured on the basis of acknowledged and well-known principles while friendship is not. The mental mappings we carry round in our heads do not include friendship networks as they do kinship genealogies. While this is true, it somewhat oversimplified the characteristics of kinship. In line with everyday thought, it assumes that who a person's kin are is obvious and that consequently the basis of kinship need not be investigated. However, as the above writers have all illustrated, kinship in fact is far more complex a phenomenon than common-sense thought would have us believe. As Firth notes: 'The whole problem of what is meant by "being a Smith", and one's precise relation to the Joneses if one's mother was a Jones, is more complex than may at first appear' (1956,

p. 16). The key issue is the fundamental difference between, on the one hand, the distinctive features of kinship and, on the other, the kinsman as a person (Schneider and Smith, 1973, p. 9). It is the latter, or rather the relationships that develop between kinsmen as persons, which are of most concern in the chapters that follow, and indeed in most other kinship studies. Yet an analysis of the kinsman as a person depends on first knowing who a kinsman is, i.e. on the distinctive features of kinship.

Following Schneider, we can recognise that in Western culture there are two bases of kinship: blood and marriage. Kinship is accepted as being dependent upon these principles, with kin being defined by them. A 'blood' relationship is formed by a single act of sexual intercourse in which the sperm provided by the male reacts with the egg within the female to create a new being, their child. The child's natural mother and father are given and fixed for ever at the time of the procreative intercourse. All a person's blood relatives are consequential on, and given by, acts of sexual intercourse which result in birth. All those who share a natural ancestor can be characterised genealogically as blood relatives. As Schneider and Smith write of American kinship: ' "Blood" is thus a state of shared physical substance. This shared physical substance is, in this culture, an "objective fact of nature", a natural phenomenon, a concrete or substantive part of nature. And this objective fact of nature cannot be terminated' (1973, p. 10).

Whereas blood relatives are seen as part of the given order of nature, relatives by marriage are seen as part of the order of law which is imposed by men through their own customs and habits. Marriage, while recognised as being culturally natural to members of the culture, is not seen as part of the order of nature. It is a human construction and a social arrangement, a way in which people order their social world. Consequently as a principle of kinship it differs from blood in that it can be terminated and changed. It is because marriage is social and consequently fragile that blood is in the end recognised as being the more important of the two principles on which kinship is based. Indeed it can be argued that the major reason marriage becomes a principle of kinship is because it is the institution in which legitimate procreation occurs.

However, to argue in this way, to suggest that kinship is ultimately about biology and nature, is to run the risk of assuming that our ideas about nature are themselves natural. Whatever the ultimate truth of currently held genetic theories concerning human creation, the views accepted in our culture about kinship in general and specifiable kin in particular are merely ideas and beliefs, and as such social constructions rather than natural and invariable facts obvious and apparent in themselves. In the end our knowledge of kin is derived from conventional assumptions which, because they are shared, work for all practical purposes. Thus when we examine the matter we can recognise that in reality our kinship system is not based directly on ascertained, or even ascertainable, fact. Not only are very few of us capable of specifying with any precision how 'blood' is passed from one generation to the next but, crucially, there is no way of demonstrating conclusively who one's kin are. In the end these issues matter little as, apart from rare cases of litigation over hereditary rights, they do not affect our social being. For all intents and purposes we can accept that those people who are acknowledged by all to be our natural kin are indeed our natural kin. None the less it demonstrates that kinship is a social interpretation of natural phenomena rather than the natural phenomena themselves.

While most of the time we can assume that 'social kinship' corresponds with 'natural kinship' there are occasions when we know it does not. That is, occasions on which the social behaviour involved in a relationship is that of kinship but where there is no tie through blood or marriage. There is some ambiguity over whether such relationships should be considered kin ones. For example, while people who have been adopted are recognised as having all the legal status of natural children, respondents frequently regard it as necessary to report the fact that others are adopted in giving genealogical information, presumably because they are thought of as qualitatively different from children attached directly through nature. Similarly are step-mothers and step-fathers kin? Is a long-term cohabitee of a kinsman to be regarded as kin in the same way that a legal spouse would be? If so, is a short-term cohabitee to be regarded similarly? Such issues as these point to the fact that kinship is not as given or as objective as it first appears, for in these ambiguous cases it is the social relationships existing as much as theoretical conception of kinship that determine whether or not a 'kin' relationship is recognised and honoured. Biological and legal 'fact' provides a working model, but this model needs to be adapted in social practice.

The social bestowal of kinship is important in another respect: that of kinship structure. Although the legal and biological model underlying genealogies is capable of indefinite extension, it is in practice limited by selection. As Firth (1956) and Williams (1963) have noted, while the number of others recognised as kin by English members is larger than is commonly assumed, it none the less tends to be smaller than the number recognised by members of many non-Western societies. Essentially, compared to other kinship systems, the English one is characterised by shallow genealogical depth but relatively full lateral extension within generations. The most important feature of the English kinship system, however, is the variation found within it. Not only is there considerable variation in the

THE NATURE OF FRIENDSHIP AND KINSHIP

range and number of kin claimed and known (see Firth, 1956; Williams, 1963; Firth *et al.*, 1970) but the actual relationships that are maintained between specific categories of kin vary a good deal. This is so with respect both to different respondents and to genealogically similar kinsmen of the same respondent. Thus for example not only do the sociable relationships that different people maintain with (say) their first cousins vary, but typically any individual's relationships with his various cousins also differ. Indeed, recognising the existence of a genealogical relationship need not necessarily involve behaving towards that person as a kinsman. As Williams notes, "just as every individual has an unique set of *actual* kin so too does he have his own unique view of which persons do or do not constitute his kindred and of their particular relationships' (1963, p. 152). It is because of these features that Firth has characterised the English kinship system as permissive rather than obligatory (1956, p. 14).

In summary, our culture provides us with a formal model based on the twin principles of 'blood' and 'marriage' which can be extended indefinitely for ascertaining who kin are. In the normal course of things this model has the appearance of being fixed and precise, of being given by the rules of nature and law. Upon investigation, the application of these rules is more precarious than we customarily think. Their solid appearance depends on social convention and the ecology of on-going relationships. The correspondence between kin given by the model on the one hand (Schneider's distinctive features of kinship) and those people we recognise as kin on the other (his kinsman as a person) is not as obvious as we normally assume. It is because of this imperfect correspondence that kinship can be said to be socially bestowed and accredited.

The problem this leaves us with is knowing exactly who kin are. As we have seen, it is impossible to specify kin totally through appeal to biological and legal facts as these are assumed rather than known definitively. Yet kinship is clearly about these biological and legal facts. This conundrum has given rise to fascinating debate in anthropological circles (see Gellner, 1957, 1960, 1963; Needham, 1960; Barnes, 1961, 1964; Beattie, 1964) but need detain us no further. For the present purpose – that of contrasting kin and non-kin relationships as they affect patterns of sociability – we can side-step this issue and assume that kin are those people whom respondents recognise as kin on the basis of their knowledge of the dual criteria of kinship: blood and marriage. We can accept our informants' views of the world and, following Thomas's famous dictum, take kin relationships to be those they define as such. For our purposes the truth or falsity of their models can be held in suspension. This indeed is the practice commonly adopted in most empirical studies of kinship interaction.

Thus, bearing the above points in mind, we can accept that normally for members of our culture the rules of blood and marriage provide the framework by which kinship issues are understood and decided upon. They are the only criteria for assessing whether someone is kin or not. In the end other criteria are seen as irrelevant. In particular the type of relationship you have with a person can of itself never be a legitimate substitute in the absence of ties of blood or marriage. Someone may be treated as kin but if there is no belief in a blood or marriage connection by accepted definition they are not kin. Conversely no social relationship necessarily develops simply because people are recognised as having some connection through blood or marriage. In other words, kin labels are for our purpose *categorical* labels. So in many respects are labels such as 'workmate', 'neighbour' or 'colleague'. They all serve to locate people in the social structure in sets of categories with others similarly placed on the basis of criteria that are, to a degree, independent of the personal relationship that exists between them. However, as with kinship, there is an element of social recognition and bestowal involved with these relationships too. Which particular individuals are actively recognised as, say, neighbours or workmates in part depends on the strength and character of the social relationships one has with them. Assuming they satisfy the external criteria, those who are known best will be labelled more surely as neighbours or workmates (or what have you). For neighbours the subtleties of these processes have been analysed nicely by Williams in his study of Gosforth (1956) and by Stacey and her co-workers in their studies of Banbury (Stacey, 1960; Stacey *et al.*, 1975). Indeed Banbury's gentry provides one of the most extreme demonstrations of the basic principle here for they 'did not define as their neighbours those who lived physically next door to them, but only those of a similar social status living in other parts of the county' (Stacey *et al.*, 1975, p. 103).

FRIEND RELATIONSHIPS

When we consider friendship we can recognise that it is of a different order from categorical relationships. Factors external to the on-going relationship play no part in its definition. The term 'friend' is only applied to people who have a personal relationship that is qualitatively of a particular sort. It is the actual relationship itself that is the most important factor in deciding whether someone can or cannot be labelled a friend. Thus as well as locating people in the social structure, the term friend also implies something about the relationship between those so labelled. Thus it is a *relational* label rather than a categorical one. To express this more graphically, if one imagines gathering all a person's kin together, or all his neighbours or all his colleagues, there is no way of knowing what type of relationship (if any) he actually has with any of them. If all his friends gathered together, on the other hand, certain rather general assumptions could be made about his relationships with them. Indeed this is tacitly recognised in some of the sociological research into friendship. In these reports, the specification of the nature of the personal relationships between friends is often less important than an analysis of who these friends actually are: colleagues, neighbours, workmates, fellow club members or whatever. But in kinship studies, for example, the opposite applies; these studies are almost always concerned with analysing the nature of the on-going relationship between people who happen to have been defined as kin.

If this were the end of the matter, the analysis of friendship patterns would be comparatively simple. On this basis, all friend relationships should be of a similar kind, so all that needs to be done is to specify what that kind is. Unfortunately there are further complications. While the concept 'friendship' refers to a particular kind of sociable relationship, it is one whose definition is by no means precise. The range of relationships that can be covered by the term is great. Various connotations, not all of which occur in concert, can be brought into play at different times and on different occasions. So in everyday speech the concept is used to express different aspects of what we take being a friend to mean. In one context we may use the term to signify someone we are very close to, a 'true' or 'real' friend; elsewhere someone we have only interacted with in a handful of sociable or leisure situations may, in passing, be referred to as a friend.

A number of sociologists and anthropologists have recognised the difficulty there is in defining friendship. Julian Pitt-Rivers, for example, responding to his own question 'But what is a friend?' wrote: 'The range of interpersonal relations between Aristotle's axioms and the jejune imperatives of Dale Carnegie lead me to wonder' (1961, p. 182). Naegale, too, has recognised the wide variation there can be in friend relationships (Naegale, 1958). What is surprising is the number of sociologists who either fail to recognise the variation there can be in the meaning of the term, or who, having recognised it, fail to take it into account in their analysis. After reviewing a selection of sociological literature on friendship, Edgell is quite right to reflect that: 'In none of the studies referred to so far has the meaning of friendship been adequately conceptualised by the investigators. It is a case of making excuses or measuring the extent of a social phenomenon without giving prior thought to what is being measured' (n.d.).

The difference between 'being friends' and 'being friendly' is recognised readily enough: the former involves some degree of personal knowledge and some sense of mutual communion, and the latter merely assumes a form of attitude that follows from acknowledged rules of propriety and allows interaction to proceed smoothly and without risk of upset. (Indeed, Burns pointed out that one can even be friendly with people one dislikes, calling this the 'polite fiction'; 1953.) However, having made this distinction, many writers assume that being friends is an invariable, and therefore unproblematic, state of affairs. Frequently only the most intense forms of friendship, those between 'real', 'true' and 'very close' friends, are considered. If a relationship is not characterised by strong emotional attachment, feelings of empathy, mutual sympathy and understanding, it is immediately classified as something other than full friendship and removed from consideration. This is most evident in much of the quasi-philosophical writing on friendship. In this, the dictates of Aristotle are taken as the defining criteria of any friendship worthy of the name. Unfortunately the same is true of some of the sociological 'theorising' about friendship. To some degree, Ghurye (1953), Schmalenbach (1961), Kurth (1970) and Sadler (1970) all make this kind of assumption.

However, within sociology the tendency to treat 'real' friendships as *the* form of friendship is more pervasive in another guise. In empirical studies respondents are often asked to name their 'best friends' or those to whom they feel closest. Various questions are asked about these friends and from the answers the researcher extrapolates and analyses friendship in general. Obviously in such cases the range of relationships that will be included in the analysis is severely limited because of the paucity of the sample of friends about whom questions are asked.

Examples of this process are prevalent in the research literature. Lazarsfeld and Merton (1954) base their influential discussion of value and status homophily in friendship formation on the results of an interview in which respondents were asked questions about their 'three closest friends'. Robin Williams, in his study of friendship and social values, recognises clearly the problems there are with the category 'friend', but nevertheless proceeds in his analysis on the basis of questions about: (1) his respondents' best friend in their immediate residential area; (2) their best friend in the larger urban area; and (3) their best friend living anywhere. From these questions it is surprising that Williams is able to distinguish two types of friendship, one being 'marked by diffuseness, collectivity-orientation, norms of affectivity, and a relatively high degree of affective involvement' and the other tending 'to be specific, self-interested, oriented to norms of affective-neutrality, and low in affective involvement ("commitment")' (1959, p. 78). Babchuk and Bates asked their respondents – middle-class married couples – to name their 'very close mutual friends' (1963, p. 378; also see

Babchuk, 1965). Similarly Zena Blau lists three questions she asked of her elderly respondents in order to ascertain 'the extent of (their) friendship participation'. The first asked them how many 'really close friends' they had in the town; the second how often they saw 'the friend that [they knew] best here in town'; and the third whether they thought of themselves as '(going) around with a certain bunch of close friends' (1961, p. 430, footnote 4). As a final example, Booth and Hess, for their analysis of cross-sex friendship, asked their respondents to think of those non-kin people they thought of as friends and then asked them to list those 'persons you would consider to be your very closest friends' (1974, p. 40).

These examples – and others can be found to support them – all illustrate the emphasis there is in the literature on extreme forms of friendship. Although a lot of what has been written generalises about friendships of all forms, the data it is based on usually pertain to a restricted set of very close friends.

There is a further consequence which follows from friendship being a concept that is imprecise and variable which also has important bearing for research into friendship patterns. This relates to the way in which respondents use the term. To put the matter simply, if the concept 'friend' has various connotations and strands of meaning, it is important to know exactly which of them a respondent is using when he discusses his relationships with his friends. If there can be a degree of conceptual variation, the researcher must come to understand the ways in which each of his respondents uses the concept in the interview situation. At an everyday level the meaning may be taken as obvious, but for research purposes the obvious must be treated as problematic. It is particularly useful to discover why someone is not regarded as a friend, especially in those numerous cases where respondents are not quite sure whether the person they are discussing can or cannot be regarded as one. The point to make here is that in common usage terms like friend (and mate, pal, chum, etc.) are only vague means of analysis; they serve as resources as well as restraints. People use them as labels and devices for conveying meaning in particular situations, not as rigorous and precise analytical tools. This must be borne in mind when we come to interpret what respondents report.

ASPECTS OF FRIENDSHIP IN WESTERN CULTURE

In the remainder of this chapter I want to explore some of the main elements involved in our concept of friendship. The 'data' I shall use in doing this come from two sources: (1) previous sociological analyses of what friendship comprises; and (2) the accounts of their friendships given by the Selden Hey respondents. These sources will be used interchangeably. It is legitimate to use other researchers' writings in this way because not only have they expended time and energy in analysing the concept 'friendship' as their own informants have used it, but also they (like myself) are members of Western culture and, thus, to a fashion, 'experts' in the meaning of the term. It is of course equally legitimate to use other cultural material as data in this way, (e.g. novels, plays, advice columns, diaries, etc.). I restrict myself to the sociological literature on friendship because in this the analysis of what friendship is is most explicit. Following Schneider's lead (1968, p. 13) many of the themes I develop below have been refined through discussing them informally with various 'informants' who, as above, are 'experts' on the meaning of the concepts friend and friendship.

The first point to make about friendship is that it is taken as a *personal* relationship in three connected senses: (1) that it is a relationship between individuals; (2) that it is a private relationship; and (3) that it involves the person as the person he really is (itself a cultural construct).

In the first sense friendship is a personal relationship in that it is seen as involving individuals as individuals and not as members of groups or collectivities. In other words, belonging to a particular group of people or being affiliated to them in some formal way does not lead to any other group of people being called friends. Nor does it lead to those in your own group necessarily being regarded as friends, although there is nothing to stop a group of people all being friends with one another. This follows from what was written above about friendship not being based on criteria external to the personal relationship between people but referring to the quality of that relationship.

Two points are directly related to this: first, friendship scores low on what McCall *et al.* (1970) term 'formality'. That is, friend relationships are not structured by the formal role position of those who are friends, for friendship is seen as independent of a person's formal role position. Most important, friendships do not develop between people *solely* because of the role positions they fill in any organisations or institutions. Secondly, following from the idea that friendships occur between individuals as individuals, a friend is valued as a unique person and cannot be replaced as can a person occupying a formal role position (e.g. a doctor or a lift attendant). Of course friends change, with new ones taking the place of old ones, but the new friends, like the old, are interacted with on the basis of their individuality and are not (or at least should not) be thought of as particular examples of a general interchangeable set of others. In Paine's phrase, friends are not considered to be 'mutually substitutable persons' (1969, p. 513).

Friendship is also a personal relationship in the sense of it being a private one, of concern only to those who are the friends. Thus friendship follows what Simmel calls 'the principle of excluding everyone who is not explicitly included' (Wolff, 1960, p. 369). Within legal limits, what is involved in a particular friendship, what friends do together, even how they treat one another, is for them alone to decide. As Suttles (1970) points out, friends can afford to ignore the normal 'rules of public propriety' when with one another. Even if what they do together upsets the moral or legal sensibilities of outsiders, this is not a ground for criticising the friendship as a friendship.

It follows from this that, unlike blood brotherhood and some other relationships that anthropologists tend to translate into the term 'friend', friendship in English culture is not institutionalised. Although others may try to influence a person's friendship choices, there are few societal conventions governing who can and who cannot become friends. (Normally any pressure exerted over friendship choice is informal, e.g. gossip and ridicule, rather than formal, and usually only occurs when the friends differ markedly in sex, age or class.) Nor is there any ritual or public performance attached to friendship. Friendships are not formally made nor broken; there are no symbolic activities connected with these processes. Thus friendship just happens as you get to know someone, so cannot be created through ritual. And as it is of concern only to those who are friends, public demonstration of its strength is unnecessary. Friends may in fact create ritual in their friendship, for friendship is an open relationship subject to 'private negotiation' (Suttles, 1970, p. 97). They may also develop their own argot of 'shorthand' speech patterns (see Naegale, 1958, pp. 243–4) but neither ritual nor argot is necessary to any friendship.

The third sense in which friendship is personal stems from the notion that ideally in friendship people should 'be themselves', the people they 'really' are, with all pretence and pretension wiped away. (Whether or not this is actually possible is not relevant here. What is important is the cultural belief that this is how things should be between friends.) Someone who is truly a friend is not meant to put on a front or an act, he is taken as someone who is genuine; who, while with friends, is natural. To get to know someone as a friend involves getting to know the 'real person'. To like them is to like this 'real person' (Naegale, 1958; Kurth, 1970; Suttles, 1970).

Now some friends will (that is, will be allowed to) get to know and understand a person's 'real self' better than others. This will make them better or closer friends. This aspect of being *allowed* to get to know the real person is important, for, referring back to Simmel, it is the means by which the individual has control over who is explicitly included. Only those whom he allows an opportunity to witness and view part of the (presumed) unadulterated natural self will be considered, or will consider themselves to be, friends.

Thus friends should be admitted to what Goffman terms the 'back-stage' or 'back-region' (1959) of one's performances, for ideally friends can be trusted not to reveal to others what they learn there. In many ways Bates's analogy of the person's self occupying a series of rooms which he allows others to view is more apt here (1964). Not only are some friends allowed to see more of the dwelling/person than others, but also in practice 'rooms' may be revealed to different friends in a different order. In other words, Bates's analogy more fully captures the potential variations and processes involved in revealing one's 'real self' to others. To claim that some friends are allowed to discover the 'real self' more than others is to say that some are trusted more than others. This is the major difference between those people labelled 'real' or 'true' friends and the remainder. 'Real' friends appear to be trusted totally and can be relied on to protect their friend's interests. It is recognised that they will not reveal or use revelations of the self meant for their ears alone. Other friends not labelled real or true ones are likely to be treated more cautiously, only being permitted to visit some rooms, and then perhaps for only brief periods. They are people who are found interesting and with whom one is sociable, but they are not people to whom one reveals innermost fears or worries. As Suttles (1970) develops at length, an important way in which people become friends, and 'everyday' friends 'real' friends, is by breaking the normal 'rules of public propriety'. This serves to reveal the 'real self' and for the friends symbolises the strength of their friendship bond.

A second characteristic of friend relationships is that they are defined as voluntary. They are seen as consequent on the free choice and selection of each friend by the other. To put this another way, they are achieved rather than ascribed. Where there is a personal relationship with another based on criteria other than free choice, or when a person's choice is consequential to a greater or lesser extent on factors for which he perceives he is not responsible, then the relationship is unlikely to be considered one of friendship.

This brings us back to a point made earlier. Relationships which arise from people's formal role positions are unlikely to be thought of as friendships if those concerned see their interaction as being consequent more on their formal role position than on the exercise of free choice. To say this is not to deny that friendships can, in fact, occur between people who occupy formal role positions vis-à-vis one another. Indeed this is one of the most common sources of friendships and, as Suttles remarks, in formal organisations friendship plays its part by providing 'a means of going beyond prescribed institutional or organisational affiliations' (1970, p. 97). It is to assert that whether a friendship is made or not is up to the individuals involved and is never a *necessary* consequence of their interaction in their respective role positions.

That ties of friendship and kinship are often seen as mutually exclusive in Western culture would also appear to be related to the notion that friends are achieved rather than ascribed. I have suggested above that friendship refers to a quality of the personal relationship existing between individuals whereas kinship is based on criteria external to that relationship. Consequently it would be reasonable to assume that a kinsman could be a friend, just as a colleague or a neighbour can, as there is nothing contradictory or mutually exclusive in the terms. However, such analytical distinctions are generally not made in everyday life nor in much of the sociological literature, so that in practice kin tend to be seen as distinct from friends. Only when people are asked specifically about the nature or quality of their relationships are they apt to describe kin as friends (and then as 'best friends'). Thus C. Turner reports that 'Kinsfolk . . . are never recognised as merely friends' (1964, p. 215) and similarly Naegale (1958), on the basis of discussions with high school students, points out that kin and friends occupy different spheres of activitiy. Schmalenbach (1961) goes so far as to suggest that kinship and friendship have an entirely different basis, the former being an example of 'community' and the latter of 'communion'. At a more mundane level, kin and friends are often treated separately in empirical research, not least in community studies (e.g. Mogey, 1956; Stacey, 1960). Babchuk and Bates (1963), Babchuk (1965) and Booth and Hess (1974) amongst others similarly operationalise friendship in such a way that kin are explicitly excluded. The same distinction is tacitly assumed by many anthropologists when, for want of a more appropriate term, they equate relationships found in other cultures in which kin are explicitly excluded with friendship as it exists in our culture.

An assumption entailed in the idea that friendship is voluntary is that it is a relationship based on enjoyment. A friend is someone with whom you enjoy spending time and sharing activities. That is, a friend's 'real self' is appreciated and enjoyed for its own sake. Conversely if you do not enjoy interacting with someone, they are unlikely to be considered a friend. In some ways, though, to say friendship is a relationship of enjoyment overstates the case, for the enjoyment is implicit rather than explicit. It could be described as a relationship characterised by 'enjoyment by default'. Usually it is only over specific activities – a dinner party, an outing together – where a particular effort has been made by one or both sides that friends actually express enjoyment. For more mundane everyday interaction, it is unusual to do so. Because in our culture friendship is entered into voluntarily it is reasonable for those involved to assume that the other(s) are party to the interaction because they enjoy it.

The matter is complicated by the fact that enjoyment in interaction can come from two analytically distinct sources, only one of which is directly tied with friendship. First of all interaction may be enjoyed because the people involved like each other and, quite simply, enjoy interacting with each other no matter what the activity in which they are engaged. The relationship is enjoyed for its own sake. But interaction may be found enjoyable for another reason. The enjoyment may stem from the activity more than from the relationships those involved have with one another. For example, one may enjoy playing football or singing in a choir, but does this make one's fellow football players or choristers friends? In part the answer depends on how well they (their 'real selves') are known. Ambiguity arises when some are known quite well within a particular social context but are not interacted with outside that setting. On the one hand, not only have such people been selected from the rest of the group present, apparently for their personal qualities, but further the activity itself is freely chosen, defined as social and presumably found enjoyable. On the other hand, in McCall *et al.*'s phrase, these relationships are none the less 'embedded' in a given social structure. To this extent they are not chosen freely but are almost equivalent to the more formal role positions the individual occupies. It just happens that these people are in the choir too, or in the football team or whatever. Frequently in the interviews, the Selden Hey respondents were unsure whether someone could be called a friend because of the basic contradiction. Similarly Naegale's groups of high school students created the concept 'just a friend' to cover this ambiguity, i.e. to describe people who were more than acquaintances but with whom interaction only took place within the structured, given (and therefore not freely chosen) setting of the school.

In general, the reasons why people become friends are treated as unproblematic in our culture, except in that branch of it known as psychology. It is something that just happens, and apparently just happens naturally. It cannot be forced or contrived. It may be encouraged, with an effort being made to develop it – in the words of one respondent who was beginning to get to know a colleague as a friend: 'We're working on it' – but to be thought of as genuine it must not be forced. Interestingly there are virtually no myths prevalent in our culture to 'explain' friendship attractions. There is no equivalent to what may be called the 'we-were-made-for-each-other' syndrome or to the mystical 'chemistry of sexual attraction' that are sometimes found in accounts of relationships of love. Nor is chance given as a reason for friendship because friendship is a relationship over which the individual is accepted as having some control. While it cannot be contrived it has to be facilitated. The individual could stop the process before it became friendship. You meet people by chance, live near them by chance, even work with them by chance, but you do not form a friendship by chance. If you ask a respondent why X or Y is a friend, the most common answer is 'I don't really know'. Occasionally more positive answers are given, such as: 'Well, we share the same interests.' But such answers are recognised as insufficient as clearly others who also share the same interests are not regarded as friends. More rarely other, apparently fuller though in fact equally vague, answers are given. For example, one respondent replied to such a question about one of his friends: 'Our characters seemed to mesh like two cogs.' In English culture, then, friendship is taken as not needing explanation. There just happen to be some people whom you come to regard as friends. Why this should be so, why you in fact get on with them, is not questioned.

Another important aspect of friendship that is emphasised in the research literature is that it should be non-exploitive. It is not a relationship *formed* for instrumental reasons, but one that exists simply because it is found to be enjoyable. It should be undertaken for its own sake rather than for some ulterior motive or as a means to some other end. Unlike Reina's (1959) portrayal of friendship among the Ladinos for example, in our society friendship is not a relationship created solely for the favours that can be obtained through it. Its *raison d'être* is not to gain political or economic advantage nor to secure oneself against possible future misfortune. Indeed little is more likely to destroy a friendship than one person perceiving that another is using their relationship solely in order to obtain some extraneous benefit from himself.

This does not mean, of course, that friends do not exploit their friendships, nor that they get nothing out of them. As Paine points out (1969, p. 506), Wolf (1966) is wrong to assume that a friendship is *either* expressive *or* instrumental. This is illustrated nicely by the work of Burridge (1957) and Pitt-Rivers (1963), even though both are dealing with friendships in other cultures. Friends can quite legitimately make use of one another in instrumental ways without threatening the relationship, provided that it is clear that they are being used because they are friends and not friends because they are useful. Thus a friend would expect to be used if he could help in some way but would feel less charitable if he discovered the other only treated him as a friend so that help could be obtained from him. One way in which the image of the relationship as one not being *based* on instrumental or exploitive intersts can be sustained is by an effective or putative *equivalence of exchange*. That is, if A asks his friend B for help in some task, he does so on the implicit understanding that B in turn could use him at some future time. It is so that friendships can be seen to be non-exploitive that the ideas of reciprocity and symmetry are so important to them. The idea is best captured by Naegale when he talks of 'infrequent reciprocity' (1958, p. 244), for in friendship the reciprocity must remain implicit and this is achieved best when it is an informal, almost casual reciprocity.

A major means by which reciprocity is maintained in friendship is by the person who last benefited seeking to redress the balance. It works out as a case of the 'debtor' seeking to repay more avidly than the 'creditor' seeks to claim, for in this way the former can show that their relationship is not one of exploitation but one of friendship. Individuals find it embarrassing to be continually asking for assistance or receiving services of one form or another but never getting a chance to repay them. For example, a number of Selden Hey respondents reported that they did not like asking a friend X to babysit as X never needed their services as a babysitter in return. Perhaps X was childless or had a mother who babysat for her. The consequence was the same. The respondents did not want to put themselves in continual debt to their friends even though the friends themselves might not mind.

Closely tied to the idea of reciprocity is the notion that friendship is a relationship between equals. In Edgell's terms (n.d.), it is a symmetrical relationship with the parties to it not being differentiated in an hierarchical manner. Within the context of the friendship no side has more authority or greater status than the other. It is a relationship typified by *communitas* rather than structure (see V. Turner, 1974). This is one reason why friends tend to occupy the same status in the wider society as one another, a theme developed by Lazarsfeld and Merton and one as true for the Selden Hey research as for previous studies. Friends tend to be of similar age, sex, class and marital status. Blau (1961) has shown the importance of these structural variables in her analysis of friendship amongst the elderly. Rosow also emphasises such variables, writing: 'Status similarities generally provide a strong basis for solidarity because they join persons of like social position who have the same relation to the larger society and who share a common set of life experiences, problems, perspectives, values and interests' (1970, p. 63). In other words, not only are people with similar status in society likely to find this consonant with treating each other as equals but further their 'real selves' are more likely to have things in common as a consequence of their similar structural position.

A final way in which friendship is a reciprocal relationship is that, in general, a friend is only regarded as a friend to the extent to which he considers you a friend. In other words, friendship must be reciprocal in terms of both sides' labelling of the other. This is a rather different kind of reciprocity from that discussed above. It refers not to the activities involved in a friendship – though it ultimately depends on these – but to the definition each person has of their relationship. The principle was spelt out clearly by one respondent who, while considering whether he regarded any of his former colleagues as friends, said: 'No, I don't think they were. I got on with them very well at work, but it was just at work . . . I'm trying to think whether any of them would call me a friend. I don't think they would, no.' Other respondents, though not stating the matter as plainly as this, recognised that people who did not regard them as friends could not be regarded as such either.

Chapter 5

Middle-Class Sociability

In this chapter I shall examine the organisation of middle-class non-kin sociability, concentrating in particular on friendship. In the chapter that follows I shall analyse working-class sociability. (See the Appendix for a discussion of the way class is operationalised in this text). The reasons for this division are both conventional and substantive. Not only have the vast majority of previous studies separated their material in this way but, more important, this division more than any other highlights the major variations that occur in the organisation of social life. In these chapters I have also followed the convention of treating kin and non-kin separately. It should be evident from the previous chapter that this is not meant to imply that friendship is seen as confined to non-kin. (However, in order to simplify this and the next chapter a little, I shall not insert the prefix 'non-kin' continually. Unless explicitly stated as not the case, whenever I refer to friends in these chapters I mean non-kin friends.)

As noted in Chapter 1, research into patterns of sociability is confined very largely to occupational, community and kinship studies. The great majority of all these sources concern themselves with working-class social life. The middle class remain remarkably untouched by sociological research. The few occupational studies which run counter to this general tendency include the Pahls' study of managers (1971), Salaman's of architects (1974), and Goldthorpe et al.'s research on routine white-collar workers (1969). In the kinship field, there have been two recent British studies specifically interested in middle-class kinship (Bell, 1968a; 1968b; Firth et al., 1970) but both of these only discuss non-kin relationships very briefly. Middle-class non-kin relationships are discussed a little more fully in the various British community studies that incorporate middle-class areas in their research (e.g. Stacey, 1960; Willmott and Young, 1967; Stacey et al., 1975). However, because overall there is a relative paucity of data on middle-class sociability this chapter will rely to a good extent on material from the Selden Hey fieldwork. (North American community studies will not be considered mainly because the rather frantic middle-class social life depicted in them, cf. Seeley, Sim and Loosley, 1956, Whyte, 1963, does not seem to be found in English middle-class culture.)

It has already been noted in Chapter 1 that the majority of research concerned with sociability supports the general thesis that the middle class maintain friendships with a far wider range of people than the working class. Studies have consistently shown that middle-class respondents tend to have more friends than their working-class counterparts. For example, whereas less than 8 per cent of Bell's middle-class respondents said they had no best friend (Bell, 1968b, p. 61), and only one of Salaman's sample of fifty-two architects failed to name five friends (Salaman, 1974, p. 105), Mogey (1956, p. 96) found that nearly two-thirds of his (working-class) St Ebbe's sample had no friends at all. Similarly, while forty-six of Gavron's middle-class housewives exchange visits with friends during the daytime (Gavron, 1966, p. 104), only about a third of Young and Willmott's Bethnal Green sample had friends with whom they were on visiting terms (Young and Willmott, 1962, p. 108). Although concentrating on the number of friends claimed is far too simple a measure, it is worth noting here that in the Selden Hey research too the middle-class respondents claimed far more non-kin friends than the working-class respondents. Whereas only one of the twenty-one middle-class respondents claimed at the time of the interview to have no friends, five of the twenty working-class respondents said they had none. Similarly, only one of the middle-class respondents said there was only one person they knew whom they regarded as a friend but four of the working-class respondents claimed this.

In addition to having a greater number of friends, the middle-class are also recognised as forming friendships with people met in a wider variety of social settings. Goldthorpe et al. reflect this theme nicely when they write about the 'propensity of our affluent workers and their wives to limit their friendship relations largely to kin *or* neighbours' (their emphasis), and compare this arrangement to that of their white-collar couples who 'draw more heavily on friends made through work and, in particular, on friends who are neither kin, neighbours nor workmates' (1969, p. 90). In a similar vein, Margaret Stacey suggests that 'broadly speaking, in working class streets near neighbours are the most important sources of friendship and of help. In the middle class, friendships outside the street are at least as important as those with neighbours' (1960, p. 104). The Selden Hey research confirmed this conclusion too, for on the whole proportionally more of the working-class respondents' friends were drawn from work and neighbour contacts. The middle-class respondents selected their friends from a wider range of settings. However, this formulation, like that of comparing the number of friends claimed, is too simple. The working-class respondents' friendships did not stem solely from these sources, and, in any case, the middle-class respondents also drew the majority of their sociable contacts from neighbourhood and work associates. The differences arose more from the way that sociable relationships drawn from other spheres of activity were organised by the working-class respondents, together with the greater geographical mobility of many of the middle-class respondents. Even though most friendships gradually lapse after a move, many middle-class respondents regarded some of those they had been friends with elsewhere as still friends. In comparison, the few people the working-class respondents regarded as friends tended to be more local, while not all were actual neighbours.

SOCIAL SKILLS

In seeking to account for this diversity in friendship patterns researchers have concentrated on the different social skills supposedly possessed by middle-class and working-class respondents. They have pointed out, quite rightly, that friendships do not occur haphazardly but are organised and constructed by those party to them. In other words, friends have to be made, they are not God-given. This process of making friends involves certain skills, for sociability, no matter how it may appear, is never formless. To put it rather crudely, a number of writers have suggested that such skills are prevalent in middle-class culture but largely absent from working-class culture. In large part this differential possession of social skill is seen as a consequence of the middle class's greater geographical mobility. Here the ultimate model is Whyte's 'Organisation Man' whose promotional spiral requires his frequent moving of home from one area of the country to another. Because they are never long in one place, he and his spouse have to be capable of making (and jettisoning) friends quickly from those they meet if they are ever to enjoy any form of sociable interaction. Both Klein (1965) and Willmott and Young (1971) explicitly refer to Whyte's prototype in pointing out the care with which the middle class make friends.

Willmott and Young write of immigrants to Woodford Green: 'The kind of people who move into the suburb, mostly into homes of their own, seem to have difficulty in getting to know each other and make friends . . . Most people, particularly the younger couples . . . seem to have the capacity to put down roots quickly wherever they live' (1971, pp. 91–2). In contrast, Gavran suggests that working-class couples may never learn 'the social skills involved in making new acquaintanceships and transforming these acquaintanceships into friendships' (1966, p. 98). Klein points to some of the skills involved in doing this: 'It takes rather a marked ability to discriminate, to perceive and use fine shades of meaning, to indicate and preserve delicate social distances if the chances of making friends are not to be impaired by a wrong move in the initial stages' (1965, p. 352). Goldthorpe *et al.* capture this emphasis on social skills when they write that their affluent manual workers 'remain in fact largely restricted to working class styles of sociability, and in the formation of their friendship relations are for the most part neither guided by middle class norms nor aided by middle class social skills . . . Actually *making* friends – through personal choice and initiative – from among persons with whom no structured relationships already exist could not be regarded as at all a typical feature of their way of life' (1969, p. 91, emphasis in original; see also Hill, 1976, p. 168).

Looking at friendship patterns in terms of social skills is at the same time both useful and misleading. It is useful to the extent that it emphasises that friendship involves organising relationships in particular ways. It points to the need to view friendship as an arrangement which is constructed through the efforts of those involved. On the other hand, suggesting that friendship is a process requiring social skills found mainly amongst the middle class implies that the working class are in some way deficient. They are seen as *lacking* the necessary skills. If only they could cultivate them, then they too could enjoy friendships just like the middle class. In other words, this approach seems to assume that friendship is a superior, more difficult form of sociable relationship and not merely one variant amongst others. It ignores the fact that friendship is a cultural construct with specific connotations and strands of meaning, as outlined in Chapter 4. Instead of analysing patterns of sociability in terms of skills possessed by one cultural group (the middle class), the approach I shall use here will concentrate on the actual organisation and development of non-kin sociable relationships.

If we turn to the Selden Hey study, without doubt the most important difference between the working-class and middle-class respondents lay precisely in this sphere. Briefly, whereas the working-class respondents tended to restrict interaction with their friends (and with their other sociable companions) to particular social contexts, the middle-class respondents developed their friendships by explicitly removing them from the constraints imposed by specific settings. That is, they expanded the rules of relevance of their relationships so as to include the possibility of interaction in a variety of contexts. This 'flowering out' of middle-class sociable relationships and their consequent independence of given social settings placed the emphasis on the individuality of those in the relationships, and thus allowed the middle-class respondents to recognise them readily as friendships. Although the evidence from other studies is difficult to evaluate because it is not presented in a similar form, a careful reading of the literature suggests these patterns may be typical more widely. Certainly there is little evidence that is not consonant with this interpretation. The fuller implications of this approach will only become apparent in Chapter 6 when working-class patterns of sociability are considered. In this chapter, though, it is necessary to specify more thoroughly than has been done previously the organisation of middle-class friendships. While what follows was derived from the Selden Hey research, there is reason enough to believe it holds true elsewhere.

THE DEVELOPMENT OF MIDDLE-CLASS FRIENDSHIPS

What I am attempting to do in this section is to describe some of the more important features that are typically found in middle-class friendships. I am not setting out a definitive path that such friendships necessarily follow, but simply attempting to illustrate the way in which these relationships were generally developed and constructed by the Selden Hey respondents. It is essential, as mentioned above, to recognise that being friends is an active process. Friendships do not just happen, but are both generated and structured by the participants. They are organised and created around the participants' knowledge and assumptions about what in general such relationships involve.

Before anyone can become a friend, that person must first be met. More than this, at the beginning of the relationship he or she is likely to be interacted with in one particular social setting. At this stage, that setting will dominate the relationship. It matters little whether the setting is work, locality, a social club or organisation, a joint recreational pursuit, or whatever. The relationship will be conceived of basically in terms of that setting. Because of this, the individuals at this stage do not see their interaction as voluntary or freely chosen. Gradually, however, through informal interaction within this setting, the interactants will get to know one another and gain insights into one another's personalities. In this way, they will implicitly make decisions about their liking for one another, what they have in common, whether they enjoy interacting together, etc. Out of the group of people met in a setting, some will be selected on these and similar criteria, and will consequently be interacted with more than others. As yet, though, none of these people will necessarily be thought of as friends. They are more likely to be conceived of as people who are seen because of the particular setting they both find themselves a part of, e.g. as neighbours, colleagues, fellow club members, and such like. In other words, the rules of relevance of the relationship are still dominated by the particular situation of their meeting.

When the middle-class respondents wanted to develop one of these relationships further, and get to know a person better, what they tended to do was to change the implicit rules of relevance from those imposed by a given situation to ones which, in effect, emphasised the individuality of the interactants and their relationship, their liking for one another and their mutual compatibility. They did this by broadening and widening the situation and activities in which interaction occurred, thereby overcoming the limits tacitly imposed on the relationship by the initial situation. In other words having got to know and like someone, or, perhaps more accurately, having come to realise through interaction in a specific setting that they would like to know someone better, the respondents changed the rules of relevance of their relationship by activating it in settings other than that in which they had so far seen one another.

Thus, people met, for example, at work or a club, or perhaps through others, may be brought home or entertained for a meal or for drinks. Alternatively, arrangements may be made to go out to a dance or to the theatre with husbands (boyfriends) or wives (girlfriends). Or perhaps those involved may arrange to play golf, say, or go to a football match together. It does not matter greatly what the activities are; the point is simply that the people are purposefully interacting in different situations with one another, and thereby altering the basis of the relationship. Organising and arranging relationships in this way allows each person to come to know the other better, and serves to emphasise the idea that it is the individual relationship, and not any given activity, that is important. To a degree, this is what 'becoming friends' means – getting to know and like the individual through interaction in various freely chosen sociable activities and settings.

The use of the home is particularly important in this, as it is the individual's private domain. The constraints imposed on interaction in externally organised settings are largely removed, and the individuals are (apparently) free to interact as they wish. At the very least, interaction in the home is likely to provide an opportunity for cues to be picked up which are thought to reveal the person as he is when he is 'being himself' in his natural habitat. Further, because such meetings are clearly consequent on choice rather than circumstances, they serve again to emphasise the desire of the participants to interact purposefully for its own sake with one another. As we have seen, all these are important elements in the concept 'friendship'.

The 'flowering out' of the rules of relevance of a relationship so as to involve activities of different sorts, and interaction in a number of settings, is typical of middle-class friend relationships. Naturally, this does not imply that the friends are endlessly engaging in new activities together. Quite clearly they are not. As is illustrated in the case examples to be given below, particular activities and settings, be they playing cards or going out for meals, or entertaining for drinks and going to dances, or whatever, emerge and routinely dominate these relationships. The point is that the relationships as they are perceived by the participants are no longer structured exclusively by the situation of their interaction. By engaging in other activities, recognising and, in a sense, legitimising the possibility of interaction in different settings, they have broken through the implicit restrictions of the rules of relevance of their original encounters, whatever these were, and replaced them by ones which emphasise their meetings as individually chosen and based on their enjoyment of interacting with one another for its own sake. I suggest that this is the single most important feature in the organisation of middle-class sociable relationships Again it must be remembered that not everyone with whom the middle-class respondents were sociable was treated like this. As discussed above, there is a process of selection before this stage is reached

Rather than giving individual examples of friendships, I shall illustrate the friendship process outlined by discussing all the major friendships of four relatively typical middle-class respondents from the Selden Hey study: Mr and Mrs Harris and Mr and Mrs Parry. In this, my aim is to show that the development and 'flowering out' of friendships is a normal, routine part of the organisation of these relationships. I will also use these 'apt illustrations' to illustrate other features of middle-class friendship to be discussed presently.

The Harrises

Mr and Mrs Harris, who were both in their mid-thirties, had lived in Selden Hey for seven years. Before that, they had lived in Birmingham. Mr Harris was a self-employed professional with a practice in the town nearest Selden Hey. His wife was a qualified librarian, but at the time of the interview was a full-time housewife and mother looking after their three young children. Two points of particular interest emerged from the Harrises' accounts of their friendships: (1) all Mr Harris's friendships are joint friendships, usually initiated by Mrs Harris; and (2) at one point they explicitly recognised that they held different conceptions of friendship.

The only people they still regard as friends and are still in contact with from before they moved to Selden Hey are Colin and Jane, and David and Barbara, both of whom they knew in Birmingham. Mrs Harris originally came to know Jane through working with her, and initially the friendship had not involved their husbands. The two females interacted with each other during their free time at work, and increasingly outside this setting, extending the scope by taking shopping trips together and occasionally visiting each other's homes.

Gradually their husbands became involved in the relationship and got to know each other well, so that the four of them became good friends. As well as visiting each other, they went out together for meals at weekends, especially before their children were born. Jane and Mrs Harris also continued to see each other at work until Mrs Harris left when she was pregnant. Since the Harrises have moved to Selden Hey the relationship has died down. Initially they wrote quite frequently to each other, and made arrangements to visit, but now they merely send Christmas cards to one another.

Mrs Harris was also the one to initiate their friendship with Barbara and David. She met Barbara at a local park where they both took their young children. This led to their visiting each other at home, while their husbands were at work. As with Colin and Jane, their husbands were gradually brought into the relationship, so that by the time they left Birmingham they visited and entertained this couple quite regularly. They also went out with them for meals or to dinner-dances on occasion, though, as at this time both couples had young children, this was not very frequently. The Harrises still see David and Barbara and their family each year for alternate visits, and exchange letters and telephone calls periodically.

When Mr Harris was discussing the friendships that they had made since coming to Selden Hey, he made somewhat contradictory statements. First of all he said that their pattern of friendship had changed dramatically. They knew far more people than they had ever done before. 'And we're still making new friends. As a rough indication, we've added about twenty people to our Christmas card list this year compared to last.' Later, however, he claimed there were really only three couples he regarded as friends, stating that the rest were little more than acquaintances. With all three of these couples they go out for meals to restaurants as well as to each others' homes, to the theatre and to dances. With two of them their main activity is playing cards. They know these last two couples – Simon and Elizabeth and Maggie and Neil – somewhat better than the third, Jim and Penny, and interact with them more frequently. Simon and Elizabeth and Maggie and Neil also know each other well, whereas Jim and Penny are involved more with another set of people whom the Harrises know only vaguely.

Mrs Harris had been the first to know both Elizabeth and Maggie. She met Elizabeth soon after coming to Selden Hey. By chance, both she and Elizabeth were attempting to start a playgroup in the village. After some initial antagonism, they agreed to combine their efforts, and found that they got along with each other very well. As with Barbara in Birmingham, they began to visit each other with their young children during the daytime. They involved their husbands in the relationship, and began interacting in the evening.

Again the main emphasis was on entertaining and visiting, supplemented by occasional meals out. After a short while, they taught Mrs Harris to play bridge and this activity is now their main pastime. The four of them generally play at least once a week.

The Harrises' relationship with Maggie and Neil is very similar to that with Simon and Elizabeth. They play bridge with them, too, most weeks, but they go out with them slightly less often. They helped introduce these couples to one another, and the six of them now form something of a group. Mrs Harris had originally met Maggie through the babysitting circle she joined when she first moved to Selden Hey. From this, their relationship developed in much the same way as did that with Elizabeth.

The Harrises are somewhat less involved with Jim and Penny than these other two couples. Mr Harris originally met Jim through their both being members of a local charity fund-raising group. They do not entertain or visit Jim and Penny as often as Elizabeth and Simon or Neil and Maggie, partly because they do not play cards. Instead, they tend to go to the theatre or to dances together, or else to go out for meals together, a favourite pastime of the Harrises.

Mrs Harris said that apart from those six people, she knew at least another fourteen in the village whom she also regarded as friends. These were mainly females she had met through the babysitting circle or through playing badminton. While her husband knew most of their husbands he did not regard them as friends. They only interacted with these people as couples infrequently, generally at parties or similar large social gatherings. They rarely went out with any of them as a foursome. While Mrs Harris said she went round for coffee with these people, and occasionally went out with them or visited them in the evening, and was inviting them all to a party she and her husband were to give shortly, she recognised that her interaction with them was much less intense than with Elizabeth and Maggie and their husbands. She said that while one of these others, Betty, was her 'best friend' and was seen most days, she was not really a 'bosom companion'. So while her relationship with these people was evidently not limited to the social context in which they first met, be it badminton, the babysitting circle or the local school, they were not as developed as the relationships that also involved her husband.

Overall, these individual friendships depended more on Mrs Harris's activities as a housewife and mother than did her friendships with Maggie and Neil, Simon and Elizabeth or Jim and Penny. If she, or they, had not been present in Selden Hey in the daytime, she would have seen little of them. It was this that made Mr Harris realise that, in discussing these relationships, his wife was using a slightly different conception of friendship from the one he held.

He said that while he had many acquaintances through his work, or his wife, or simply through having lived in Selden Hey a number of years, they were just acquaintances, and he did not really regard them as friends. He said his wife probably knew the people she was talking about better than he knew these acquaintances, but probably not as well as he would need to know people before he would recognise or call them friends.

The Parrys

Mr and Mrs Parry, who were both in their mid-twenties, bought a house on the new housing estate in Selden Hey three years before the interviews began. Before that they had lived in south London. Mr Parry works in the publicity department of a large firm in one of the nearby towns. Before the birth of their son six months ago, Mrs Parry had worked as a secretary in London, commuting daily from Selden Hey.

The people they regard as friends now can be separated into three groups: (a) those they knew when they lived in London; (b) those they have met through their work; and (c) those they know through living in Selden Hey. The majority of their friends were joint friends. They both recognised that they had kept in touch with many of their joint friends through Mrs Parry's efforts. If it had been left to Mr Parry, contact would probably have been lost with these friends.

As a child Mrs Parry lived next door to Joan and went through school with her. Even though both are now married and living a good distance apart (Joan and her husband, Pat, live in Reading), Mrs Parry still recognises Joan as one of her two best friends – the other being Mr Parry's sister. Mr Parry said he would not call Pat a 'friend' but interacted with him when their wives met, which they generally did about three or four times a year, usually in London, where their parents still lived, or for weekend visits to each other's homes. The week before one interview the Parrys had driven to Norfolk to see Joan and Pat who were staying there on holiday. Joan and Mrs Parry also ring each other up every six weeks or so.

Mr Parry also regarded a person he had known since childhood as his closest friend. Ron and Mr Parry had been in the Boys' Brigade together, and when they both lived in London had spent a lot of time together. Even after they left the Boys' Brigade, they continued to do a great deal together. Both Mr and Mrs Parry recognised that Ron was Mr Parry's friend, and, as Ron was unmarried, the relationship remained mainly an individual one between the two males. A little before the Parrys moved to Selden Hey, Ron went to America and had been there until just before the interviews started. Apart from news learnt through Ron's parents, there had been no contact between Mr Parry and Ron in this time. Now that he was back, they had met again, and apparently got on extremely well as before. 'No, there was no tension. We felt perfectly at home with each other. That's what friends are, though, isn't it?'

When they were in London, both Mr and Mrs Parry were active members of a local church. Through its youth club they got to know a number of other people with whom they kept in contact when they were courting and after they were married. The Parrys had been one of five couples from the youth club who met each month in turn at each others' homes. They were still in contact with three of these four other couples, although the regular meetings had ceased before they came to Selden Hey. As they all lived a good distance apart now they were seen rarely, usually only at Easter and Christmas when they all tried to meet at their old church. Mrs Parry claimed that if they lived nearer they would interact with these people a lot more than they do, especially with Maureen and Ted to whom they were closest.

In the second interview, Mrs Parry nominated three of the girls she worked with in London as friends, saying at the same time that their relationship was confined to work. Only now that she has left have two of them, both unmarried, come to stay for a weekend in Selden Hey. In a later interview, when talking about these three and the other girls with whom she worked and formed a lunch group, she implied that in a way they were not friends in the usual sense, but 'really just people I worked with. Because you work with them, you tell them everything that happens, even the most personal things, but they're not friends. If you'd met them outside and not at work, you wouldn't feel a lot in common with them and they wouldn't have become friends.' She went on to say that because of this, when you leave work you never see most of them again, even though they know a good deal about you.

Mr Parry no longer sees any of the people he worked with in London (three years ago), and claimed only two people at work now as friends. Ken he described as his best friend at work. They usually spend their lunch break together in the town where they work and get on well with each other, but do not mix a lot outside work. 'Ken's got a lot of interests . . . commitments, the car, sailing, various clubs. If he lived nearer [he lives 8 miles away], we would be very friendly. Apart from Ron, he's my closest friend.' The Parrys have been out with Ken and his wife Jennifer as a foursome a few times, and join one another at staff dances and parties, but the relationship is mainly between the two men. The other person Mr Parry gave as a friend was Dave, whom he sees less often than Ken and to whom he is less close. On the other hand, when the Parrys first moved to Selden Hey they went out with Dave and his wife a number of times. Since then this had died down.

When the Parrys moved to their present house, it had only just been completed, along with the other houses in the road. Consequently, because of the inevitable problems of moving into new property, they met a number of other people who had moved into houses nearby at the same time as them. Since then, they have come to know two other neighbours they now regard as friends. The first people they got to know were Helen and John. Mrs Parry travelled to London with Helen every day. And Mr Parry used to play golf with John quite frequently. They also went out to the local pub together a good deal, and occasionally out for meals. Mrs Parry said: 'Since we've had the baby, we've not been as friendly. We've not had the time really.' Her husband rejoined: 'Well, even before that we weren't really as friendly as we were.' In a later interview, Mrs Parry said she did not see 'eye to eye' with Helen. There were apparently no rows or disagreements, and they had still travelled daily on the train together, but Mrs Parry found Helen's attitude annoying: 'I can't really put my finger on it. Certainly it wasn't as strong as disagreeing . . .'

Although they never went out with them as much as with Helen and John, the Parrys got on better with Claire and Steven. Over the last three years, these four had come to know a good deal about each other. They occasionally entertained each other for a meal, though more often for a drink and a chat. Mrs Parry had made use of Claire's help with her new baby as well, and since she stopped work quite often had coffee with her in the daytime. At one point Mrs Parry said 'I hope we keep in touch with them if we ever move', a desire she did not express for any of her other neighbour friends.

Leigh and Jackie were another couple who moved into a house in Selden Hey about the same time as the Parrys. As with Helen and John, the Parrys went out with Leigh and Jackie quite regularly when they first moved. However, since then Leigh and Jackie have moved house twice, and the Parrys have now lost touch with them.

Mrs Parry used to commute daily to London with Mary as well as Helen. At this time she and Mary were really only friendly as fellow commuters. 'It was only on the train. To tell you the truth, I always thought her a bit odd. But since we've both had the babies we get on very well and see a lot of each other.' They now meet most days, sometimes more than once, for coffee or to go to the shops, or for a trip to one of the nearby towns. Mr Parry knows Mary's husband to say 'hello' to, but neither he nor Mrs Parry like him very much. 'He's a planner, even the baby . . . careful in the extreme!' Despite their frequent interaction, and Mrs Parry's recognition that she would go to Mary if she ever needed help, she said that if they moved they would probably not keep in touch, especially if they moved any distance away from Selden Hey.

The last neighbours they gave as friends were Alison and Jim, who had only recently moved to the estate. They were gradually getting to know them through having them in for drinks occasionally, and providing minor reciprocal services for each other like looking after the respective cats when one of them went away. Over the course of the interviews the Parrys interacted more and more with Alison and Jim, yet they were very aware that there were important differences between them, both situational and personality ones. 'They stay in a lot, and, although it seems a ridiculous thing to say, they seem younger. That seems to make a difference. We get on well enough, and when (Alison) has the baby we'll probably see quite a lot of each other, but there's something missing. I don't know exactly what it is . . . for example, I gave a Tupperware party the other day and you'd think as a neighbour she would come, wouldn't you? But she didn't. A very independent person really.'

It can be seen that all the friendships discussed in these case illustrations had developed in similar ways. From interaction in particular settings, the relationships had 'flowered out' and been broadened so as to involve other types of activity. There had been an explicit effort made by those involved to change the original rules of relevance of the relationships by removing the relationships from the initial social settings in which they occurred and activating them in various alternative settings. It does not matter that in most cases these alternative settings were limited; the essential point is that the original structure had been replaced by new ones. In this way the relationships were extended and developed by the participants in a manner that emphasised the individuality of the friends rather than the context of their interaction. Further, while in most cases the activities the friends actually engaged in with each other were limited (e.g. to bridge evenings, casual chatting or visits to local shopping centres), the friends recognised that potentially their interaction could occur in any number of situations. It happened that they were limited to one or two that they enjoyed doing together most, but there is no intrinsic reason why they needed to be.

To middle-class eyes, these considerations are likely to appear obvious and laboured. The process described is hardly remarkable; it is, after all, what we mean by becoming friends with someone. However, typical though it is of middle-class friendships, the process is not typical of working-class sociable relationships. As I shall show more fully later, these are developed in a different way. Instead of allowing sociable relationships to 'flower out' by adding to and changing the range of activities they undertake with others, working-class members would seem to restrict their relationships to the initial context in which they occur. They tend to develop their relationships only within the limits imposed by this setting. These themes will be discussed more fully in the next chapter. First it is necessary to look at variations in middle-class friendships.

VARIATIONS IN FRIENDSHIP

While the great majority of middle-class friendships are patterned and structured by the general principles outlined above, these patterns by no means determine the specific organisation or content of individual friendships. Within these parameters, there is a good deal of variation in the activities and sentiments encompassed in any friendship. This is evident from common experience and is illustrated in the examples given earlier. A variety of factors influence the specific format of any relationship as well as the number of friends a person has. Clearly the individual's interests and predilections are of some consequence but it is worth pointing out that such factors do not work in a social vacuum; they are not context-free. And part of this context which needs to be considered if a relationship is to be understood is the overall life situation of those who are friends, for this as much as any other factor will mould their interaction by making some activities easier to accomplish with some people than with others.

The individual's life situation structures his sociable relationships in a number of ways. At a trivial level it affects whom he meets and consequently delimits the pool of others who are potential friends. More important, the situation of the putative friends relative to one another will influence the development of their friendship. Assuming they have a desire to become friends and to extend their relationship outside the setting in which they met, such factors as the geographical proximity of their homes, their domestic arrangements, the various other activities in which they engage, their family-cycle position, their material circumstances, and so on, are likely to constrain, direct or stimulate the form their relationship takes and the activities they come to share together.

This can be seen in the case illustrations given earlier. For example, the length of time the Harrises had lived in Selden Hey, combined with Mr Harris's position as a professional in the village, had led to their having a different pattern, as well as a greater number, of friendships than they had had previously. Before moving to Selden Hey, the Harrises' married life had been spent in large towns, none of which they had lived in for more than four years. Similarly, the Harrises' frequent interaction with the three couples who were their main friends depended on their being able to get babysitters regularly, something they had always had difficulty with before. Again the Parry's relationship with, say, Maureen and Ted, and Mrs Parry's with Joan, were limited by the distance apart they lived. Had they lived nearer, the relationship would have been different. On the other hand, they had become friends with Helen and John precisely because they lived near. And, interestingly, Mrs Parry only came to regard Mary as a friend after they had both become mothers and full-time housewives. Their presumed desire for sociable interaction in their new work situation, combined with the possibility of interacting in a wider range of settings than that determined by commuting, clearly altered the nature of their relationship.

Occupational effects

One of the factors that is frequently recognised in the research literature as affecting patterns of friendship is the individual's occupation. Certainly many occupations impose constraints that structure the feasibility and form that interaction with others can take. The tradition of extra payment for anti-social hours correctly recognises this. Overall it would appear that proportionally more working-class than middle-class occupations require anti-social hours to be worked. The majority of middle-class workers are routinely assured of daytime work that will not interfere with their leisure activities or relationships. There are exceptions of course. Obvious examples that spring to mind are airline staff, commercial travellers and some military personnel. Pahl and Pahl (1971) suggest a further exception to be higher business executives who sometimes find that the demands of their work occupy most of their energies. Similarly it would seem that dual career families sometimes find the organisational prerequisites of combining two careers with running a home require that friendships are given little salience (Rapoport and Rapoport, 1971; 1976).

Generally, despite any increase there may have been in the alienation of workers in bureaucracies, it seems probable that most white-collar employment provides people with the opportunity of working with others and, thus, the possibility of initiating friendships with them. Nevertheless there are clearly differences in this respect between different middle-class occupations. Some merely provide a pool of others with whom friendships can be made and a setting in which they can be fostered. In these the work activity itself is of little moment to the relationship. In other cases the work activity may be more central, providing the occasion and rationale by which friendships are 'serviced' and kept extant. This may be especially so for those towards the higher reaches of professional life. For instance, business meetings and lunches may serve as occasions for friends to come together; conventions and conferences may provide a convenient place for friends who happen to be colleagues to meet; and in the course of their work, professionals in private practice may see friends as clients. However, there are so little data available on these matters that it is hard to draw any firm conclusions.

More certainly, we can assume that 'burgesses' and 'spiralists' have distinct friendship patterns (Watson, 1964). The geographical mobility inherent in the spiralist career results in a greater turn-over of friends than occurs amongst burgesses. With each move to a new area, new friendships are made and many, though not all, of the old ones relinquished. Two features are consequent on this. First, as both Bell (1968b) and Pahl and Pahl (1971) found, geographically mobile couples have more dispersed friendship net-works than non-mobile couples. Not surprisingly, data from the Selden Hey research concur with this pattern. Secondly, means have to be found by which new friendships can be created. There is some disagreement in the research literature over what these means usually are for middle-class couples. Bell supports Babchuck and Bates (1963) in suggesting that most friendships are initiated by the husband and that, further, he usually has the greater influence in determining who are the couple's best friends. He found that this was especially true of the geographically mobile respondents amongst his sample. In particular, the husband's work proved to be a major source of the couple's friendships (Bell, 1968b, pp. 65–6). This pattern of male dominance was not found by Pahl and Pahl in their study of managers and their wives. As they developed at length, it was the latter who initiated most friendships and organised sociability. The majority of the husbands appeared to be too conscious of their career needs to risk creating friendship obligations with people against whom they might later have to compete. As they write: 'the hierarchical nature of many organisations . . . means that colleagues are divided into those who are senior to oneself, those who are junior, and those who are potentially in competition for promotion' (Pahl and Pahl, 1971, p. 157). The number of middle-class couples in the Selden Hey sample is rather too small to pro-nounce conclusively on this disagreement. Suffice it to say that the sample revealed no consistent pattern. There were some couples, such as the Harrises and to a lesser extent the Parrys, where the wife was more influential in creating and maintaining friendships; yet there were others where the husband dominated. In general, so many situational and personality factors enter the picture that it would seem unwise to suppose that a single truth applies across the board in this matter.

The friendship patterns of wives who are 'employed' full-time as housewives and mothers raise further issues of interest here. While in a sense such people's relationships with others who are also 'employed' as housewives and mothers may be seen as synony-mous with relationships based on an external work situation, they differ in the important respect that their work setting is also their home. So if they interact with non-kin others similarly 'employed' in their homes – and all the evidence suggests that this is more typically a middle-class habit than a working-class one – they are automatically confounding the spheres of work and leisure. This has important connotations for the development of friendships because relationships that occur in the home cannot readily be characterised as situationally bound ('Oh, she's just someone at home' makes less sense than 'Oh, she's just someone at work') and also, as mentioned above, involve the person as she supposedly freely is, in her private, natural setting. Interaction in the home is also likely, as it is the individual's private preserve, to encourage a greater intimacy, partly through the difficulty of (perhaps literally) hiding one's dirty washing from the other's scrutiny. In addition, females who are at home during the daytime have more opportunity for interacting with one another than their husbands do with their friends. Because they have a greater freedom to organise and schedule their work, home-based females are more able to arrange their timetable so as to facilitate sociable interaction. Factors such as these mean that middle-class housewives' 'work relationships' are more likely than their husbands to be conceived of as friendships, for other labels are less appropriate. It is likely that both Mrs Parry and Mrs Harris held more 'liberal' definitions of friendship than their husbands because they were involved more than them in these relationships. Their husbands' work relationships were removed from the home setting and thus not 'contaminated' by it to the same extent. For them, the friend/non-friend distinction was easier to maintain.

Other factors are also at work here. For example, numerous studies have highlighted the mundane and boring nature of housework (e.g. Gavran, 1966; Oakley, 1974). In addition to being viewed by many as unproductive and hence of lesser value than 'real', gainful work, in its privatised form it entails long periods of social isolation. In these circumstances the need for support from others similarly placed in the employment structure would seem to be paramount. As there are no formal work relationships that can provide this support, informal relationships have an increased significance. According to many researchers, most notably Young and Willmott in their study of Bethnal Green, female kin fulfil this role for working-class housewives (Young and Willmott, 1962; Rosser and Harris, 1965). In middle-class culture friends appear to be more important. Pahl and Pahl (1971) postulate that whereas for the managers they studied work provided the chief focus of personal identity, for their wives friends were the main source of identity support.

Life-cycle position

One feature not yet discussed that can be expected to cause variations in middle-class friendship patterns is life-cycle position. As
this is a central component structuring the individual's situation,
interests and experiences, it will influence the number of sociable
relationships a person has and the activities engaged in with these
people, though perhaps not the organisation of these relationships
as relationships. The literature on changes in friendship patterns
over the life-cycle is surprisingly sparse. Rapoport and Rapoport's
recent publication (1975) provides some data on sociable activities
though not as much as one might like. In many ways the two most
interesting stages for present purposes are those that produce most
constraint: the child-rearing and the retirement stages. (A further
issue of interest, adolescent friendships and peer groups, is too large
and complex to be dealt with in this volume.)

I have already discussed how employment as a full-time housewife and mother affects friendship patterns. Caring for small
children inevitably involves tasks which are for the most part
repetitive, time-consuming and socially isolated; yet at the same
time it provides more opportunity than many occupations for
organising periods of sociable interaction with others similarly
employed. A further feature is also of importance in the child-
rearing or, as Rapoport and Rapoport (1975) have aptly termed it,
the 'establishment' phase. After marriage and the birth of children
the domain of sociable interaction for middle-class couples is typically domestic rather than external. The home, and the homes of
friends, replace commercial establishments as places of entertainment. Partly this is because of financial constraints – the normal
middle-class career pattern results in least money being available
when it is most needed (see Bell, 1968*b*) – and partly because of the
difficulty of obtaining regular babysitters. In addition, as children
grow up, it is likely they will make increasing demands on their
parents' leisure time. Leisure pursuits may thus become family-
oriented with resources being devoted to familial rather than extra-
familial relationships. In fact this is only partially the case as the
establishment phase appears to be the one in which the most
friendships are initiated. In part this is a consequence of the high
level of geographical mobility associated with this stage in the
middle-class life-cycle. Further, children in fact may be instrumental
in new friendships being formed, as was the case with the Harrises.
(Also see Willmott and Young, 1967; Pahl and Pahl, 1971.) In
addition, the constraints encouraging entertainment in the home
are likely to result in others being recognised as friends, for interacting with people in a domestic setting allows the rules of relevance
to alter away from those given by external settings towards ones

which emphasise the individuality of the interactants' relationship. As we saw earlier, this is an important element within our cultural concept of friendship.

Friendships are often seen as particularly significant relationships in the retirement phase of the life-cycle. This is because the elderly gradually become disengaged from more formal organisations, especially work ones, and consequently rely more heavily upon informal associations for contact with the wider society. Thus friendship is seen as a mechanism for adjustment to old age. However, empirically there is a good deal of variation in the number of friends the elderly have and the exchange content these relationships involve. Once more an appreciation of the matter is hindered by the lack of material specifically relating to the middle class.

Basically it would appear many of the patterns typical of other sections of the middle-class population apply also to the elderly. Rosow reports on the basis of American data that the middle-class elderly have more friends than their working-class counterparts and that their friends are geographically more widely dispersed (1970). Generally, the number of friends a person has declines with old age (Blau, 1961; Rosow, 1970). Contact is lost with some through disengagement from formal and informal activities and in other cases death or infirmity severs the friend bond. Even without infirmity, entertaining or visiting people for more than short periods of time can become increasingly tiring for the elderly. In addition Blau found that changes in either marital or employment status affects friendship patterns. She suggests that any change that 'places an individual in a deviant position among his age and sex peers and differentiates his interests and experiences from theirs is likely to have an adverse effect on his friendships' (1961, p. 438). Thus to be widowed or retired before most of one's contemporaries, or to work or be married longer than them, disrupts the balance of equality important between friends (see Chapter 4) and results in the individual's friendship network shrinking.

THE BREAKING OF FRIENDSHIP

In the case illustration of the Parrys' and the Harrises' friendship patterns presented earlier, it was evident that after both couples moved to Selden Hey their previous friendships altered quite radically. Most of them had gently atrophied and died, and the majority of those that were still extant were now of minor consequence. (An obvious exception is Mrs Parry and Joan). This was typical of the majority of the middle-class respondents' relationships with those they had known before undergoing a major situational change such as moving house or changing jobs. Despite most of the literature being concerned more with the making than the breaking of friendship, it is also a pattern that is consistent with previous research. As mentioned earlier in this chapter, both Bell (1968b) and Pahl and Pahl (1971) report how their geographically mobile respondents developed new friendships on moving to a new area and allowed many of their previous ones to lapse. This general tendency is consonant with what was stated above about the content and form of a friendship being affected by factors in the external situation of the friends. In general, the more radical the change in the situation of the friends, the greater the constraints against their friendship continuing.

Moving house is amongst the most disruptive influences most people experience. If the Selden Hey respondents are at all typical, the proportion of friends most people attempt to keep in touch with after a move is small. Even with these there is difficulty in maintaining contact for more than a year or two. Initially letters are written and visits may be arranged, but in most cases these soon drop off until eventually even that most celebrated symbol of remembrance, the Christmas card, is not sent. In general, long-lasting friendships are comparatively rare, although a minority of respondents claimed one, and occasionally more than one, 'real' or 'true' friends whom they had known for quite long periods. However, friendships of this type are not at all typical, despite most quasi-philosophical discussions of 'the nature of friendship' treating them as though they were.

Friendships can also end for other reasons, of course. The example of the Parrys with Helen and John illustrates this. Here the relationship which developed when the couples moved almost simultaneously into new houses in the same road had gradually petered out and become less active. Being neighbours, the two couples still met and were friendly with each other, but the bond of friendship appeared to be dissipating as a result of attitudes being found increasingly irritating and different interests emerging. The dissolution of friendship in this way can be even more gradual and less dramatic than the throwing off of ties that occurs after a move. Nevertheless, it is probably common to a number of friendships. As one's interests and status change, those people who were once close may be found less convivial and compatible than before. A similar process is found with some would-be friendships in that while attempts are made to become friends by widening the rules of relevance of the relationship, these attempts lapse after a short while as neither side finds interaction with the other as rewarding or enjoyable as they first supposed they might.

The extent to which friendships are sloughed off as one's situation and status change can vary a good deal. In the Selden Hey research, some respondents were more adept than others at maintaining friendships despite a low level of face-to-face interaction.

For example, Mr Cullen, a senior civil servant, had managed to maintain a large number of friendships from all periods in his life. He was unusual in this and was also exceptional in that he claimed more friends than any other respondent (over ninety, in fact). Differentials in the extent to which members of the middle class manage to maintain friendships are also noted in Bell (1968b) and Pahl and Pahl (1971). Nevertheless, the most significant point to make about the breaking of friendship is that for the majority of people most friendships die completely once face-to-face interaction lapses. In this respect friendships are very different from most kin relationships. In particular, as we shall see in Chapter 7, sibling relationships, which in some respects are the kin relationships most equivalent to friendships, rarely break down completely.

'REAL' AND 'TRUE' FRIENDS

During the Selden Hey research, the terms 'real friend' and 'true friend' were used spontaneously by a number of respondents in describing special friendships. In the final section of this chapter I want to consider these relationships in some detail. For this I shall depend heavily on the Selden Hey data, but will not restrict myself to the middle-class respondents. The relationships covered by the terms 'real' and 'true' friend are equivalent to some of those discussed under the rubric 'best friend' in other studies of friendship. It is important to recognise, however, that they are not equivalent to all of them. Whereas the label 'best friend' tends to be imposed by researchers in order to make their respondents differentiate clearly between 'friends' and 'acquaintances' (see Chapter 4), the label 'real' or 'true friend' is used unsolicited by respondents to emphasise the quality of particular friendships. The differences will be evident from what follows.

The first feature to note about real or true friendships is that they frequently continue even though face-to-face interaction is rare. Whereas other friendships dissipate when the friends' situation alters radically, these friendships persist. As their labels suggest, for those involved such relationships are a paragon of friendship; the emphasis in them is on the remarkable compatibility and affection those involved have for each other. The respondents saw them as transcending the need for regular contact, although, naturally, such contact is valued when circumstances permit it. Bell gives two very apt examples of this kind of friendship (1968b, pp. 66–7) and points to the importance of non-face-to-face communication for maintaining them. Mr and Mrs Parry's friendships with Ron and Joan respectively also illustrate these processes.

Salaman writes that the railwaymen in his sample, despite having fewer friends in total than the architects with whom he was comparing them, 'invested the best-friend relationship with an almost sacred significance' (1974, p. 105). This statement would seem to be true of real friendships generally. It also suggests an over-representation of this type of friendship amongst working-class respondents. While the number involved is very small, this pattern was evident in the Selden Hey research. Of the thirteen respondents who referred to one or more non-kin others as true or real friends, five were working class. Proportionately this is more than would be expected if the remarkably skewed distribution of friendships generally is considered. In addition, nearly half the working-class respondents regarded one (or more) of their siblings as real friends (see Chapter 7).

Real friendship can be seen as an extension of more ordinary friendships. Its properties are those of the latter, only more so. This applies especially to the trust and openness evident in these relationships, an aspect emphasised by a number of the Selden Hey respondents. For instance, one said of a real friend now dead: 'We were real friends. Not just letter writing friends, but real, true friends. We could say anything to one another, shout and be as rude as we wanted to, but no offence was taken.' Two important features of true friends are implicit in this statement. First, in some senses, these friendships are experienced as inalienable (see Cohen, 1961). And secondly, in them the symbolic significance of breaking the normal 'rules of propriety' is particularly strong. This theme of trust being generated through jointly breaking normal rules was echoed by another respondent who said of a real friend now returned to America: 'We used to have a lot of fun together . . . We used to get up at four in the morning and be off on the farms poaching rabbits. We got into no end of trouble!'

Another theme of these special friendships is that they are seen in some respects as analagous to family ties. Again this can be illustrated by the comments of some of the Selden Hey respondents. One said of two such friends: 'They're almost like members of the family. They come on holiday with us each year when we rent a large house for all the family.' Another said of the male workmate who helped her get over her sister's death: 'He was a *real* friend. He was was just like a big brother to me.' A third said she regarded her real friend's family, on whose farm she had worked for nearly thirty years, as 'a second family to me'. These statements again imply the inalienable character of real friendships, for elementary family relationships are rarely severed. Further, likening the relationships to family ones also emphasises their strength, for involved in them are many topics usually restricted to close family.

In summary, it is evident that these real friend relationships are qualitatively different from most friendships. While these latter gradually fall by the wayside when face-to-face interaction ceases, real or true friendships continue, and continue to be important to those involved. But it should be borne in mind that the differences are really only ones of degree. They are based on the fact that in what the respondents came to think of as real or true friendships, the liking, compatibility and sense of communion of the friends, and their enjoyment of their interaction, whatever the setting of that interaction routinely is, is greater than it typically is with most friend relationships. This, together with their continuing despite relatively little face-to-face interaction, sets them apart from the more usual, more mundane 'workaday' friendships.

Chapter 6

Working-Class Sociability

As discussed at the beginning of the last chapter, working-class respondents consistently claim fewer friends than their middle-class counterparts. Whilst it is not always easy to make direct comparisons, as different researchers rarely ask the same questions, all the available evidence supports this view. This remarkable uniformity, so rare in sociology, has not been contradicted by any study of friendship patterns as far as I know. (See, for example, Mogey, 1956; Stacey, 1960; Young and Willmott, 1962; Klein, 1965; Willmott and Young, 1967; Goldthorpe et al., 1969; Brown et al., 1972; Brown et al., 1974; Salaman, 1974; Stacey et al., 1975; Hill, 1976.) This alone would suggest that friendship as a sociable form is a more integral feature of middle-class culture than of working-class culture. Other findings support this contention. In particular, it is interesting that many working-class respondents appear to experience difficulty in deciding on the appropriateness of using the label 'friend' for describing their sociable relationships. After reviewing an extensive selection of the relevant research, Klein writes: 'Friendship is a category of social behaviour which does not fit easily into traditional working class life and hence its definition presents difficulties both to the social investigator and to those whom he questions about it' (1965, pp. 137–8). Similarly Mogey, in quoting his St Ebbe's respondents, demonstrates their hesitation to use the term 'friend' to describe their non-kin relationships (1956, pp. 94–5).

In the Selden Hey research, too, the working-class respondents not only claimed fewer friends than the middle-class respondents but also had much more difficulty in deciding whether somebody could be called a friend or not. Whether the label was an appropriate one for a particular relationship seemed to trouble them far more than it did the middle-class respondents. The working-class males overcame this difficulty by describing others as 'mates' rather than, and as distinct from 'friends'. Because of its male connotations, their female equivalents could not use this term to the same extent, so had to find other means of expressing their ambiguity. 'Well,

I'm not sure what you'd call her. She's not really a friend, at least not what I'd call one' was a fairly typical statement from them.

The fact that these respondents maintained sociable relationships of some importance with people they were hesitant to call 'friends' points to the problems inherent in relying on friendship counts. It makes apparent the fact that claiming X or Y friends is not equivalent to claiming X or Y sisters, say, for numbers cannot be compared in the same way. The character of the relationships and the implied meaning of the terms used by respondents to describe them require understanding before any valid comparisons can be made. Even then making such comparisons probably has little value as it is difficult to demarcate the categories of relationship one is comparing. At their boundaries, the grounds used to decide that one relationship is important or significant enough to be included in a numerical comparison but another not are inevitably haphazard and vague.

In any case I would argue that contrasting the number of friends claimed by middle- and working-class respondents serves only to conceal more significant differences in their friendship patterns. It emphasises an epiphenomenon at the expense of underlying cultural distinctions in the sociable habits of the two groups. Certainly the Selden Hey research suggested that differences in the organisation and character of non-kin sociable relationships were more important than simple differences in the number of friends or mates claimed. That is, class-related differences in the rules of relevance the respondents constructed and applied to these relation-ships, especially concerning the areas of social activity in which they allowed them to develop, were more significant than these other, more readily measured factors. While the scale of the Selden Hey research makes generalisations hazardous, this conclusion appears to be consonant with much of the data of friendship patterns reported in previous studies.

Essentially the thesis to be argued here is that whereas the middle class develop their friendships through recognising the possibility of interaction in a variety of social settings, the working class tend far more to limit their sociable relations the particular social contexts and structures. They do not allow them to 'flower out' in the way the middle class do. The consequence of this way of con-structing and organising sociable relationships for working-class members is not that they have no 'friends' in the sense of important sociable contacts, but that their friends tend to be situation-specific. This itself makes the label 'friend' problematic, as I shall demon-strate later. So in contrast to other researchers who suggest that the working class draw their friends and associates from a limited range of received social settings (e.g. neighbouring and work ones) the point to be stressed here is that interaction with others, rather than friendship formation itself, is limited to particular contexts and settings. The various issues this raises will be discussed at length below: first though it will be useful to survey the existing literature on working-class sociability with this thesis in mind.

PREVIOUS STUDIES

The dominant image of working-class sociability portrayed in the sociological literature of the late 1950s and early 1960s was based extensively on contemporary studies of traditional working-class areas. The proto-typical working-class individual was taken to be a member of a relatively close-knit group of kin, neighbours, workmates and drinking companions. His (or her) sociable life was seen as embedded in and dominated by this tightly knit group with whom a varied range of social activities was undertaken. For females, this group largely comprised kin and neighbours, while for males it consisted mainly of workmates, especially if he lived and worked in an area dominated by an 'occupational community'. The well-known research studies conducted by Dennis, Henriques and Slaughter (1956) in Ashton, by Bott (1957) and Young and Willmott (1962) in London and by Tunstall (1962) in Hull were particularly influential in sustaining this image of working-class sociability. The essence of their portrayal is captured very nicely by David Lockwood in the discussion of traditional working-class life in his famous paper 'Sources of variation in working class images of society'. He writes: 'Workmates are normally leisure-time companions, often neighbours, and not infrequently kinsmen. The existence of such closely-knit cliques of friends, workmates, neighbours and relatives is the hallmark of the traditional working class community. The values expressed through these social networks emphasise mutual aid in everyday life and the obligation to join in the gregarious pattern of leisure, which itself demands the expenditure of time, money and energy in a public and present-oriented conviviality . . .' (1965, p. 251).

While this stereotype of traditional working-class sociability has been most influential, its validity is called into question by recent evidence and, indeed, by a careful reading of earlier research. To put it bluntly, the image of gregarious conviviality in varied contexts appears to be rather extreme if not actually false. Some of the most relevant critiques of the above view have come from recent studies of occupational communities. The linking of working-class traditionalism with occupational communities such as dockworkers, miners and shipbuilders, was of course a key factor in the production of an image of sociability that emphasised the existence of cliques of workmates, kin and neighbours.

In his recent discussion of this issue, Hill (1976) suggests that there are two ways in which membership of an occupation may be linked to patterns of sociability. First, there is the pattern implied by Lockwood in which work associates are carried over into leisure activities. But, secondly, it may be that because of the occupational structure of the local area, leisure companions in the main *happen* to be employed similarly to oneself. Here they are not selected as companions because they are workmates – indeed this bond may be rejected as a basis for sociability just as it was by Goldthorpe *et al.*'s affluent workers (1969) – but chosen on other criteria that make their like employment incidental. As Hill writes: 'In the first case it is the work place and occupation which matters, while in the second it is the outside community which is important' (1976, p. 164).

Hill's distinction here is of crucial importance for understanding patterns of sociability as the first view clearly contradicts the idea that working-class sociable relationships tend to be limited to particular social settings, while the second is compatible with it. Hill's own work on London dockers clearly supports his second interpretation. While 47 per cent of his sample of dockers claimed to see a lot of other people from the industry outside work, only 23 per cent said they saw much of the people with whom they actually worked (1976, p. 164). Although Hill does not analyse the data in these terms, it may well be that a proportion of this 23 per cent in fact saw their work associates outside work simply because the latter lived in the immediate vicinity of the respondent. More definitely, Hill reports that most of the social contact with these people was casual or semi-casual, over 90 per cent of it occurring in pubs. In addition he notes that few of his respondents entertained docking friends in the home (1976, p. 164).

Hill's results here illustrate, in his words, 'just how little spill-over there is of work into leisure' (1976, p. 165) amongst his sample. While his data certainly negate the traditional image of working-class sociability, the questions he asked his respondents were such that it is difficult to know if their patterns of sociability were organised along the principles suggested above. However, in the absence of more positive material, we can note that his analysis does not contradict the thesis that working-class sociability tends to be restricted to given settings and received social structures.

The study of shipbuilders on Tyneside conducted by Brown and his associates concurs with Hill's analysis in questioning the validity of the commonly held view of traditional working-class sociability (Brown *et al.*, 1972; 1974). They report that 75 per cent of their respondents claimed to have one or more 'good friends' in the shipbuilding yard where they worked. Most of these relationships appeared to be more than 'workmate' ones in that 69 per cent of the respondents with one or more good friends interacted with them

WORKING-CLASS SOCIABILITY 73

outside work, over half of them more than once a week. However, the majority of the respondents involved met these associates *only* in a pub or in a working men's club. Indeed only 30 per cent of Brown *et al.*'s respondents reported meeting workmates in other places. Although it is again impossible to draw precise conclusions from this, we might expect at least some of this interaction to be consequent on residential circumstance rather than being purposefully organised. Certainly, as with Hill's sample, it would appear that sociable interaction tended to be limited to particular social contexts, and in a number of cases may well have been a result of people happening to be regulars at the same local pub.

In all, Brown *et al.*'s 193 respondents provided information about 655 others with whom they spent their spare time (Brown *et al.*, 1972). While 45 per cent of these friends (Brown *et al.*'s label) were usually met in a pub or working men's club, a surprisingly high proportion, 43 per cent, were usually seen in the home. However, because of the way the data are aggregated it is impossible to tell what percentage of the respondents entertained non-kin at home. Indeed it is unclear whether or not the 655 others included kin. So again, while the data published by Brown and his associates contradict the usual assumptions made about working-class sociability, they neither refute nor directly support the thesis to be developed below.

The evidence from other occupational studies is even more difficult to evaluate. For example, while Goldthorpe *et al.* suggest their affluent workers have different sociable networks from their wives' and rarely entertain non-kin at home (1969, p. 92), they do not discuss the internal organisation of their sociable relationships in any detail. Similarly, in their discussions of railway-workers and lorry-drivers respectively, Salaman (1974), and Hollowell (1968) provide little material which relates directly to the issues raised here.

A number of community studies are a little more helpful, though here too the material included is often inconclusive either because of the questions initially asked respondents or because of the form of analysis adopted. Overall two conclusions emerge which suggest that working-class respondents confine their sociable relationships to given contexts. First, as with Goldthorpe *et al.*'s sample, it has been found repeatedly that members of the working class rarely entertain non-kin at home. (See Mogey, 1956; Stacey, 1960; Young and Willmott, 1962; Klein, 1965.) As discussed earlier, it is partly through entertaining others at home that the middle class change the rules of relevance of a relationship from those given by the initial context of interaction. Secondly, the above thesis is supported indirectly by the fact that most studies have found that non-kin neighbour relationships remain very much bound to the neighbourhood. Knowing someone well as a neighbour does not result in their being included in a range of sociable activities. As Klein writes: 'The oft-expressed belief that women spend a lot of their time "popping round next door" to mere neighbours receives little factual support' (1965, p. 134). (This may be less true of more socially isolated rural areas than of urban ones. For example, Williams, 1956, and Frankenberg, 1957, suggest that neighbours frequently make unheralded visits to one another's homes in the communities they studied. However, it is difficult to assess from these studies the degree to which such visits are between 'mere neighbours' or neighbours who are also kin to one another.)

The occasional passage in some community studies offers more direct support for the idea that working-class sociable relationships are contained within particular structures. Stacey, for example, writes: 'Working class husbands rarely bring their workmates home. Even when workmates are also neighbours it by no means follows that they will spend leisure time together. If they meet at all outside work it is usually only in the pub' (1960, p. 114). Even more interestingly, Young and Willmott quote one of their respondents as follows: 'I've got plenty of friends around here. I've always got on well with people, but I don't invite anyone here. *I've got friends at work and friends at sport and friends I have a drink with*' (1962, p. 108, emphasis added.) Later, in discussing the pattern of social life on the new estate at Greenleigh, they imply very strongly that it is not social skills but the desire to become involved in friendships as such that is lacking. They support Lupton and Mitchell (1954, p. 70) in suggesting that the working class limit relationships to something less than friendship in order to control the demands that can be made upon them (1962, pp. 147–50). Presumably a major method of limiting relationships is to contain them securely within a given structured context.

Although Willmott's respondents in Dagenham appear more willing to use the label 'friend' than most working-class respondents, the pattern of friendship he describes seems basically similar to that found elsewhere. The relationships he analyses also seem restricted in their range. Thus, while there is a comparatively high level of home-visiting, Willmott is at pains to point out that this visiting is not equivalent to middle-class 'entertaining'. 'Most meetings inside people's homes take the form of "popping in" for a chat or to give or to receive day-to-day aid . . . The friendships that bring wives, and to a lesser extent husbands, into each other's homes are of a piece with the day-to-day meetings in the garden or street' (1963, pp. 59 and 61). Similarly the sociable relations of the male respondents seem remarkably curtailed by middle-class standards. Further, the language used by his respondents to describe friendships seems stilted and formalised and, in Klein's expression, 'sound(s) unusual to the middle-class ear' (1965, p. 138). Although once again more detailed comparison is impossible because of the form of the analysis, we can note that in this study too, like those already discussed, the picture that emerges implies that sociable relationships tend to be limited to specific activities.

There are three conclusions that can be drawn from this review of the literature on working-class sociable relationships. First, the typical working-class pattern of such relationships is clearly distinct from the typical middle-class pattern. From the material examined in this and the previous chapter, the two classes certainly appear to develop their sociable relationships differently. However, secondly, the dominant pattern of working-class sociability is in reality somewhat removed from that assumed in the literature on 'traditional' workers. In particular, the model portrayed by David Lockwood in the passage quoted earlier seems to be an idealised one. The third conclusion, which must be drawn more tentatively, is that while there is only limited positive support for the thesis that working-class sociable relationships tend to be restricted to particular contexts, there is even less evidence that is dissonant with it. Admittedly it is impossible to make comparisons with total confidence because of the different modes of analysis used in previous research, but the overall impression generated from reading this literature is that limiting interaction to specific settings is an element of some importance in working-class non-kin sociability. In addition, this interpretation of working-class sociability helps resolve the noted paradox that working-class respondents can be sociably active yet have few friends. It can also explain their reticence in using the term 'friend'. These factors in themselves suggest that organising relationships in the way outlined earlier may well be typical. Certainly it is worth discussing further. To add some flesh to the skeleton of argument presented so far, it will be useful to specify in more detail exactly what is meant by claiming that working-class members tend to limit and restrict their non-kin sociable relationships to particular, given social structures and settings. To this end, I shall provide brief examples taken from the Selden Hey material. As in the last chapter, these will be used to illustrate the analysis that follows. First I shall provide details of three of the relationships categorised by the working-class Selden Hey respondents as friendship ones. Then I shall give brief accounts of all the non-kin sociable relationships – be they considered friends or not – of two of these respondents.

THE SELDEN HEY MATERIAL

I shall begin with a comparatively active working-class friendship. Mrs Clegg claimed to have had three friends, all of whom she met through work. Two of these moved from Selden Hey on marriage and have not been seen for a number of years. The third, Chris, lives opposite her now, and works part-time with her, cleaning local offices. Their relationship was one of the fullest of those recognised by the working-class respondents as friendships. Though they knew each other as neighbours previously, Mrs Clegg and Chris only became friends through working together. They now interact outside as well as inside their workplace. Outside work they do not often visit each other just to be sociable; rather their interaction consists of such things as walking to the shops with each other, or 'popping over' to pass on some news or gossip over the doorstep. Occasionally, at weekends, they go to a local fete or jumble sale together. Thus, generally, Mrs Clegg sees her non-work meetings with Chris as having a specific purpose, but often this purpose is relatively minor, and simply provides a convenient opportunity for interaction.

More typical of the working-class respondents' friendships was that of Mr Hewitt and one of his ex-workmates, whom he regarded as his only friend. The two of them had become particularly close through working together. (It was Mr Hewitt who said of this friend: 'Our characters seemed to mesh like two cogs.') Until Mr Hewitt retired, they had only ever interacted in their work situation. After his retirement they wanted to keep in touch with each other and, as they could no longer do this through work, chose to do so by occasionally visiting each other's homes with their wives. But their interaction now, by middle-class standards, was still extremely limited. Typically the two couples chatted and told each other what they have been doing over a cup of tea. It seems that this was all that was entailed. The rules of relevance they had constructed for the relationship did not involve them in any other aspects of each other's lives. The rules emphasised maintaining contact in this way but did not encompass their meeting in other situations except by chance.

The final example of working-class friendship, one which I shall discuss in a little more detail, concerns two men, the respondent, Mr Thompson, and Len White, who have known each other for over fifty years. Until two years ago they lived in the same small village, but then Mr Thompson moved into a council house in Selden Hey, some 4 miles away from his previous home. Mr Thompson expressed some ambiguity over Mr White's appropriate status in the interviews, at times calling him a 'friend' but at other times referring to him as a 'mate'. Nevertheless, a number of important features about the way the working-class respondents constructed their non-kin sociable relationships are evident in the organisation of this relationship. According to Mr Thompson, the two of them had known each other since they were teenagers and in their youth had always 'hung about together'. Still he stressed that since they were married, the only times he ever saw Len was either 'on the road', (Mr White being a road-cleaner and Mr Thompson an agricultural worker who often had to drive the tractors from one part of the farm to another), in the pub, or when he went to buy vegetables grown by Mr White in his garden. The pattern of pub meeting was particularly interesting, for although they and their wives had gone to the same pub every Saturday night for a number of years, and had always sat with one another and spent the evening talking to each other, both Mr and Mrs Thompson saw this simply as a consequence of the two couples being in the pub together at the same time. As far as they were concerned, they did not really arrange it, it just happened that way. Their behaviour since moving supports their interpretation of this, for in the two years since they moved Mrs Thompson has only seen Mrs White once or twice purely by chance. As she said: 'We were never really friends. We were just with our husbands.' In the two years since they moved, they have never visited the Whites as a couple, nor, significantly, been back to the pub. When their association with the pub ended, so did their relationship as a foursome, as well as Mr Thompson's and Mr White's association as drinking companions. Mr Thompson still went up most weeks in summer to buy vegetables, and of course while there chatted to Mr White and stayed longer than he needed. Yet he said he would not go solely for a social visit.

It can be seen that these friendships differ radically from those typical of middle-class respondents. While there was still an emphasis on the individuality of those in the relationship – they were not simply one example of a general type, but something peculiar, special and worthwhile in their own right – this was achieved less through expanding the fields of activity seen as relevant to the relationship than by changing it from one type of activity to a restricted other type or by getting to know and trust someone *especially* well as a person within the confines of a particular situation.

Thus consider Mrs Clegg's friendship with Chris. Even though this friendship is amongst the more active of the working-class respondents', it can still be seen to be more limited in the range of arranged sociable activities defined as relevant to it than was the case of the middle-class friendships discussed previously. Mrs Clegg's sociable interaction with Chris took place in what can be conceived of as a framework of non-sociable activities. While there was clearly a flowering out of this relationship in terms of the closeness and feelings of compatibility and trust involved, there was not a similar flowering out of sociable activities. Of all the middle-class examples of friendship given earlier, this relationship is most similar to that of Mrs Harris and her friends from badminton and the babysitting circle. It must be remembered that Chris was Mrs Clegg's only extant friend, rather than being one of a number. Similarly Mr Hewitt's friendship with his ex-workmate and Mr Thompson's with Len White had not flowered out in anything like the way that normal middle-class friendships routinely do. When those sociable relationships which the working-class respondents did not label friendships are considered as well, this feature becomes by far the most important for understanding the differences between working-class and middle-class patterns of sociability. This is illustrated in the examples that follow.

Mr Grimley

Mr Grimley, who is in his twenties, lives in a council house with his wife and two young children. He and his wife have both lived in the Selden Hey area all their lives. After he left school Mr Grimley worked on a local farm, but is now employed by a local building firm. Although Mr Grimley was one of the most sociably active respondents, he denied having many friends. When the topic was raised at the end of the first interview, he said: 'I don't really think I've got many *friends*. I've got lots of *mates*, but not really friends.' He maintained this distinction between friends and mates throughout the interviews, claiming only to know two people he could call friends. When, in the third interview, I asked what the difference between the two categories was, he replied after a little thought: 'Well, a mate's someone you have a drink with or play football with. A friend's someone you can go to if you're in trouble.' This definition of friendship is rather different from that implied by most of the middle-class respondents.

It was evident from his discussion of his relationships that his category 'mate' had a number of components. In particular, while most mates were not friends, not all those he interacted with who were not friends were mates to the same extent. He said that of the people he was presently working with there were two, Ron and Doug, whom he would call 'mates', but a lot he would not. These others were just 'workmates', i.e. literally people with whom he happens to work. However, his interaction with Ron and Doug, like that with the workmates, is limited to the work situation. Though he likes them more and gets on better with them than the other people at work, this has not resulted in their being interacted with in other settings.

A number of other people met previously through work had also been regarded as mates in this way by Mr Grimley. For example, after leaving the land, he had worked for a distant cousin, Bob Jones, whom he described as 'a good mate. We weren't like boss and worker. More mates. We used to go for a drink and things

like that a bit.' Mainly, though, their interaction was at work, with
the occasional drink at lunchtime, or straight after work, symbolis-
ing and illustrating the comparative equality of their personal (as
distinct from formal work) relationship, and their compatibility
and liking for one another (despite their age difference of some
twenty years). Similarly, he later worked for three brothers, two
of whom, Stan and John, he regarded as mates and with whom he
got on well at work, though not seeing them outside the work
setting except by chance. The third brother, Dave, was one of the
two people Mr Grimley called a friend. Although, as with Bob
Jones, there was a large age difference between them as well as a
formal employee–employer relationship, Mr Grimley said very
emphatically that Dave was a friend. This appeared to be because
of the trust generated in the relationship rather than because of any
explicitly organised sociable interaction. Even when they worked
together their interaction outside work was minimal, mainly being
restricted to an occasional drink when work had finished. Now
that Mr Grimley worked elsewhere it was even less frequent. But for
Mr Grimley this was beside the point. As he said: 'I could go to
him. Put it this way, if I was in need of something and Dave had
it, he would lend it to me.' Later, when her husband had gone to a
darts match, I asked Mrs Grimley whom she thought her husband
would go to if they were in a financial crisis, and she replied:
'Dave.' Before his step-father or brother? 'Yes. Dave and him
are real good friends. He could turn to Dave.' While Dave is in a
better financial position than either Mr Grimley's step-father or
brother, it is interesting that Mr Grimley's definition of a friend
is supported by his wife's statements here.

Mr Grimley said there were four people at The Blue Cow, the
pub he went to, whom he would call 'mates'. 'I know most people
in there to talk to, and play darts with, but these four are a bit
special.' As with the people at work, the situations in which he
interacts with these four are the same as with the others, i.e. the
pub and the Sunday League football team drawn from its customers,
but the four he recognises as 'mates' are differentiated from the rest
because of the personal relationship that has developed between
them over the years. Like Mr Grimley, these four go to The Blue
Cow four or five times a week, and generally meet each other and
form a group, together with Steve (see below), and Mr Grimley's
brother. Apart from the pub and its associated activities there are
no other situations in which Mr Grimley interacts with these four,
except when by chance he meets them in the village. However, a
fifth member of the group, Steve, was the other person Mr Grimley
regarded as a friend. He said Steve was 'quite a good lad. I'd call
him a friend.' Of the group in the pub Steve was the only one,
apart from his brother, whom Mr Grimley sees outside the pub

setting and arranges to meet. He said: 'Steve sometimes calls round and says "Come on out for a drink" . . . Sometimes we go and watch a game of football together . . . And quite often I use some of his equipment at work.' He also plays darts and football with him (as he does with the four mates). While Mrs Grimley knew all the wives of these five to chat to when they happened to meet in the village, she was not sociably involved with them more actively. The group was very much a male one based on the pub and the sporting and social activities deriving from it.

Mrs Marsden

Mrs Marsden also lived on the council estate with her husband and teenage daughter. She is in her forties and works in a plastics factory some 4 miles from Selden Hey. Like Mr Grimley she did not really regard the people she knew as friends but was unable to find a satisfactory alternative label. As terms like 'mate' and 'pal' have male connotations, she tended to make statements like: 'I'm pretty friendly with X' or 'Well, she's not really a friend, but I get along well with her'.

There are three people Mrs Marsden is particularly friendly with: Audrey, Jean and Deidre. Audrey now lives a few doors up the road from Mrs Marsden, but they have known each other since they were children. While they only go out together rarely – and then only to one of the nearby towns shopping, or to a fete at the local church – they chat and talk to one another quite frequently. As her husband laughingly said – to Mrs Marsden's obvious embarrassment – 'Aye, the two of you are always spreading a little bit of scandal around.' Mrs Marsden said she would 'pop round' to Audrey's to borrow any household item she needed, but that they rarely went into each other's house. 'I have been in her house but we don't make a habit of it.' Nor did they interact together in any externally organised sociable settings. Their meetings were restricted to chatting in the street and on the doorstep, and to the occasional shopping trip.

Mrs Marsden has also known Jean for many years, through their both living in the village and through their working together for a time. Jean now worked with Audrey, and it was largely because these two had become very friendly with one another that Jean and Mrs Marsden had formed a close relationship. Mrs Marsden's relationship with Jean was not as important to her as that with Audrey but was as limited. An interesting difference, however, was that Jean and Mrs Marsden entertained each other in their houses. Because Jean did not live as close to Mrs Marsden as Audrey, she could not be chatted to or gossiped with as readily, so interaction had to be arranged more explicitly. In this case, this involved Jean and Mrs Marsden (but not their husbands) visiting each other some

Saturday afternoons for a cup of tea and a chat. Audrey was not included in these get-togethers. Apart from the occasional shopping expedition, usually with Audrey, planned interaction did not occur in, and was not defined as relevant to, any other context.

The factory that Mrs Marsden now worked in employed some sixty women. While she knew most of these sixty to different degrees, she was especially friendly with one, Deidre, who gave her a lift to work each day in her car. Still, they defined their relationship almost totally in terms of their work setting. This did not mean the relationship was only of limited significance, for Mrs Marsden got a good deal of enjoyment and satisfaction from it. She felt she could confide in and trust Deidre almost as much as Audrey, and obviously differentiated her relationship with Deidre markedly from all her other work-based relationships.

Mr Marsden was not involved in any of the above relationships. He was involved, however, in the two neighbour relationships which, apart from Mrs Marsden's with Audrey, involved purposeful interaction. The two of them had a cup of coffee most Sunday mornings with Jack and Nell who live next door to them, but otherwise only saw them as neighbours, over the garden fence and in the street. Similarly, the majority of their interaction with their other next-door neighbours, Bill and Pat, occurred through their seeing each other, by chance, quite frequently. However, very occasionally (twice in the previous year), the two couples went out with each other to see a show at the theatre in a local town. This was the only organised sociability between them.

DISCUSSION

These examples help illustrate the claim that working-class non-kin relationships tend to be restricted to particular social contexts and settings. As we saw earlier, when middle-class persons find they like someone, the tendency is, other things being equal, for them to interact, or at least recognise the appropriateness of interacting with that person in a variety of settings. This 'flowering out' stage is most important in middle-class friendship formation as it means that the relationship is not constrained by external structures. Overcoming these implicit structures, interacting with people in different situations and sharing various experiences with them are significant elements in middle-class conceptions of how one's more important sociable relationships should be organised. This is not the case with working-class sociable relationships, especially, though not exclusively, those given labels other than 'friendship'. These tend far more to be confined specifically to particular contexts. The rules of relevance applied to them are drawn more narrowly and interaction is limited to a particular type of activity and a particular setting.

Consider Mr Grimley's relationships with his mates in the pub. As he said, these people were 'a bit special'. Nevertheless, apart from Steve, whom he termed a friend and with whom he was more involved, they were only met through activities associated with The Blue Cow pub. He never arranged to meet them in other settings, nor tried to involve them in other aspects of his life. Similarly, his mates at work, Doug and Ron, while differentiated from the rest of his workmates, were only interacted with in a work setting. No attempt was made to broaden the rules of relevance of their inter-action by taking it out of this setting. The same is true of the three friendships discussed above and of Mrs Marsden's more important sociable relationships. Compared to the middle-class respondents' organisation of such relationships, these were very much limited to the initial context of interaction.

The essential issue here concerns the social construction of non-kin relationships. I am arguing that the way these relationships are normally developed in working-class culture differs markedly from the typical middle-class pattern. Instead of flowering out, working-class relationships tend to remain embedded in particular contexts, usually that of the original meeting. Those involved see each rela-tionship as relevant only to a given social setting and accept the limits imposed on their relationship by this setting. In other words, just like the middle class, working-class members select particular individuals for apparently personal reasons from the sets of people with whom they interact and treat these people as special and different from the remainder. Yet unlike the middle class, they do not attempt to extend the boundaries of their relationships with these individuals by including in them activities unconnected to the initial setting of interaction. Many middle-class sociable relation-ships are, of course, also limited to given social structures, but not the ones they regard as important. For the working class, even their more significant relationships tend to be defined in terms of specific contexts and settings. However, it would be a mistake to think that because this is so, these relationships are only equivalent to the ones the middle class leave in a structured setting and define as not particularly important. As the examples of Mr Grimley's and Mrs Marsden's sociable relationships illustrate, this is not the case. Relationships can be restricted to particular settings and still be of considerable moment to those involved.

There are two aspects to this argument. I suggested above that the middle class tend not to limit their sociable interaction to a given sphere of activity, nor define their relationships in such a way. These two elements, the *organisation* and *definition* of sociable relation-ships, while in fact clearly related to one other, are analytically separate. What distinguishes working-class sociable relationships from middle-class ones is not just that interaction is confined to a particular social setting but that the manner in which these relationships are conceived ensures that this is so. That is, the organisational differences are matched by conceptual differences which are, if anything, even more marked. The rules of relevance which shape sociable relationships emphasise the personal relationship whatever the social setting in which it occurs for the middle class, but affirms the primacy of the interactional setting in which the relationships develop for the working class. In other words it is not solely that interaction between the middle class and their friends continually occurs in a variety of settings, while that between the working class and their sociable companions does not, but that the former recognise the possibility and appropriateness of interaction in various settings while the latter conceive of and define the fields of activity in which interaction can occur as limited. Thus, in the examples given above and in the previous chapter, it could be argued that the Harrises' relationships with their joint friends, Simon and Elizabeth and Maggie and Neil, were in actuality almost restricted to interaction in one type of setting (their homes) as Mr Grimley's relationships with his pub mates are to The Blue Cow. The crucial difference, however, lay in the rules of relevance constructed by these respondents about the activities that could be considered appropriate to the relationships. For the Harrises the main activity, playing cards, did not define the relationships but was an (enjoyable) expression of them, while for Mr Grimley the pub setting did define the relationship and was seen as its *raison d'être*. In the latter case, if for some reason either side's association with the pub ended, so evidently would their relationship. From the way the relationships were described and defined, this was not at all evident in the former cases. If they could no longer play cards together, the assumption tacit in their statements was that the relationships would continue in some other form. As I explained in the last chapter, this in fact usually appears not to happen. Instead, friendships gradually die down when people's circumstances change. But this is not the point. Conceptually the middle-class respondents defined the activities they undertook with their friends as secondary to the reality of the friendship, while the working-class respondents were much more likely to define the activities as the primary rationale for a sociable relationship existing at all.

Thus the working-class respondents in the Selden Hey study frequently claimed that sociable activities are engaged in for their own sake and not directly for the sake of interacting with particular others. Unlike the middle-class respondents who emphasised planning and taking part in social activities so as to see specific friends, the former tended to claim that their meeting with others, while often regular and frequent, was not really planned or arranged at all. It was seen more as the unplanned consequence of simply being in the same place or taking part in the same activity as one another. What these respondents were suggesting was that such things just happen to work out the way they do, in general denying that they made any effort to manipulate circumstances to ensure that they did. People just happen to be there regularly, doing the same things as you were doing. Although not expressed in quite these terms, this characteristic is compatible with previous analyses, which imply by default that explicit planning plays little part in working-class sociable life. In particular, discussions of neighbourhood and pub relationships, the two areas of informal sociability that dominate the literature, are noticeably lacking in reference to interaction being purposefully arranged (Young and Willmott, 1962; Wilmott, 1963; Klein, 1965; Brown et al., 1974; Hill, 1976).

The relationship between Mr Thompson (and his wife) and Len White (and his wife) discussed earlier in this chapter nicely illustrates this feature of working-class sociability. The only place in which the Thompsons and the Whites interacted sociably was their local pub. It is evident from Mr and Mrs Thompson's accounts that they never thought of themselves as going to the pub specifically to meet Mr and Mrs White (or anyone else). According to their definition of the situation, they went to have a drink. It 'just happens' that Mr and Mrs White would be there, as they had been on most Saturday evenings for the last few years. There was no explicit arrangement that they should meet, though their established custom ensured that both sides knew the other was likely to be there.

The significance of accounts like this of sociable relationships does not depend on their factual correctness; that is, on whether or not such interactions 'really' do occur by chance and without being contrived to any extent. Rather, their significance stems from the fact that this is the way they are conceptualised by those concerned. In general, by regarding meetings as 'just happening', the importance of a given setting in the definition of a relationship can be readily sustained. Conversely, by defining their activities as planned activities with specific others, engaged in as much for the enjoyment of the interaction with these others as for the activity itself, members of the middle class are explicitly emphasising the importance of their personal relationships over and above any setting in which they happen to occur.

This in part explains why working-class respondents typically regard fewer people as friends, and more as mates or 'nearly-but-not-quite-friends', and also why they have more difficulty than the middle class in saying who is and who is not a friend. While they are often vague about the exact details, they are implicitly recognising that the mate relationship does not quite match cultural notions of friendship. In particular, it differs substantially from the idealised prescriptions found in much popular theorising (e.g. Lewis, 1960; Brain, 1976). Essentially this manner of organising sociability contradicts some of the premises on which friendship is based.

For example, while mateship involves the liking and selection of particular others as individuals, the restriction of interaction to specific contexts militates against this appearing so. The more the character of the setting intrudes and defines the relationship, the less emphasis is placed on the individuality and special compatibility of the mates. The relationship is not solely about the individual qualities of those involved, as is the ideal in friendship. Instead it is structured by the setting: the given structure of this setting constrains and dominates its form and expression. In many ways the essence of friendship is captured by the term *communitas*, yet *communitas* is, to some degree, inconsistent with the idea of structure. Consequently defining a relationship in terms of a particular structure decreases the appropriateness of labelling it one of *communitas* (Turner, 1974).

Most importantly then, mate relationships deny a central tenet of friendship: that the individual rather than the activity is central. Being seen as embedded within a given social structure and as consequent on 'just happening' to engage in the same activity, it is set apart from friendship. To those in it, it appears to be a partly imposed relationship and not one created freely for its own sake. Further, while mate relationships are certainly enjoyable, the way they are defined and organised leads to an ambiguity over whether the enjoyment stems from the interaction with the particular other or from the activities involved. This ambiguity helps render the label friendship questionable.

The mate relationship also differs from middle-class friend relationships in that it can be group-based. In the plural, the term is used to label a number of (generally male) others who are seen together in the same setting and who are conceived of as a group. Thus in the illustrations given earlier, Mr Grimley referred to the group he interacted with most in the pub as his mates, and conceptually associated this group together. While he differentiated them from the others in the pub, apart from Steve he did not differentiate between the members of this group themselves. He saw his relationships to them all as very similar. To a degree, the individual members were interchangeable with one another. I am not suggesting here that Mr Grimley did not recognise psychological and personal differences between the people who made up this group of mates, but that, *in comparison with the middle-class respondents*, the way he defined his relationships with them emphasised their 'groupness' rather than their individuality.

Group sociability of this form has been noted in numerous occupational studies. It seems to be a recurrent feature of male working-class sociable patterns. Indeed it is an element partly responsible for creating the image of traditional workers being embedded in close-knit, cross-contextual sociable networks (see, for example, Dennis *et al.*, 1956). In fact, this form of sociability derives its character from interaction defined as consequent on joint participation in *specific* settings, particularly patronage of the same pub or club. The group emerges from the setting and is largely confined to it. In other words, people go to the pub (or whatever) for a drink, not simply or solely to meet particular others but sure in the knowledge that they will find people they know and enjoy meeting. It does not matter that A and B are not there tonight for C, D, E and F are (Mogey, 1956; Klein, 1965). In this way the group has an existence of its own to some extent over and above that of the people making it up. Consequently, the compatibility of particular dyads does not assume the importance it does for the middle-class respondents and their *friends*. Further, the idea that the individuals are, to some degree, replaceable by others suggests yet another reason why these people are not readily labelled 'friends'. As was mentioned in Chapter 4, friendship is a personal relationship in the sense that friends cannot be replaced. One can have more than one friend but they are not interchangeable. Ideally each has his or her own special qualities that cannot readily be substituted by others (see Paine, 1969). The group aspect of 'mateship' contradicts this element of friendship, and makes the label 'friend' somewhat inappropriate for these relationships.

Group sociability of this sort is a predominantly male phenomenon. No mention is made in the literature of females being equivalently involved in 'group' relationships with non-kin. They tend much more to interact with people as individuals rather than as members of a 'set' or 'quasi-group'. Largely this is because females are less involved than males in externally organised sociable settings like pubs or clubs. Overall, they have less access to explicitly sociable contexts in which comparatively large numbers of people come together, and consequently less opportunity to form such groups.

Partly because of the way sociable relationships are organised, working-class couples are also less likely to be involved in each other's non-kin relationships than are the middle class. Whereas the middle class typically regard other couples as their joint friends, the conceived unit of the friendship here not being the individuals but the two couples as couples, working-class sociability is more segregated (Frankenberg, 1957; Klein, 1965; Goldthorpe *et al.*, 1969). Non-kin relationships are conceptualised as involving the husband or the wife but not both. Even where interaction is joint, as with the Thompsons and Whites, the bond of friendship and the reason for the interaction is usually seen as the individual relationship between one person from each of the couples. (It does not follow, of course, that working-class couples are more segregated in other aspects of their domestic lives than the middle-class couples for, as Platt, 1969, has noted, there is no' necessary correlation between the jointness of different activities.)

There is quite wide agreement that the major sources of sociable relationships for working-class females are the neighbourhood and, if employed, their work. As with the middle class, neighbours are likely to be especially important where wives are at home caring for children in the daytime. However, the two groups of females construct rather different relationships with non-kin. It might be supposed that continual interaction with specific neighbours would lead to a different form of relationship from that described above. This is not so. With the middle class such neighbours would come to be involved in various sociable activities including entertaining or going out with each other. The evidence from previous research points clearly to working-class neighbours limiting their interaction to what can be termed loosely the 'neighbourhood structure'. Interaction might be frequent and the relationship important, yet its boundaries and what is included in it are none the less restricted.

An extreme example that illustrates this occurred in the Selden Hey survey. Mrs Knowles and Mrs Clegg had known each other since school and had lived next door to each other for fifteen years. The trust generated between them as neighbours is reflected in the fact that Mrs Knowles depends on Mrs Clegg to take care of many household needs whilst she is out at work. Mrs Knowles joked that Mrs Clegg 'spends all our money' because she pays a number of bills for them. Yet the two women only interact over the doorstep and in the neighbourhood. They hardly ever entertain or go out with each other, and neither regards the other as a friend. Clearly such a relationship is foreign to middle-class culture.

A central element in the different ways neighbourhood relationships are organised by females in the two classes lies in their use of the home. Many studies have reported that the home tends to be treated by the working class as the exclusive preserve of the family with non-kin being entertained in it rarely. Indeed, few community studies of working-class areas have failed to emphasise this point. For example, Young and Willmott write: 'Most people meet their acquaintances in the street, at the market, at the pub, or at work. They do not usually invite them into their own homes' (1962, p. 107). Similarly Goldthorpe et al. write that their data suggest 'the persistence of the long-established working class belief that the home is a place reserved for kin and for very "particular" friends alone' (1969, p. 92). (See also: Mogey, 1956; Stacey, 1960; Klein, 1965; Gavron, 1966.) One exception here is Willmott's study of Dagenham where an unusually high degree of home-visiting by female neighbours occurred. As noted earlier, however, this visiting was not akin to middle-class 'entertaining', being 'of a piece with the day-to-day meetings in the garden or street' (1963, p. 61).

This exclusion of non-kin from the home is compatible with a limitation of sociable relationships to particular social contexts. As was noted in the previous chapter, a major mechanism by which the middle class transform the rules of relevance of relationships away from those implied by particular activities is through entertaining in the home. This practice serves to demonstrate for them that their interaction is based on friendship and is not solely consequent on their both happening by chance to pursue the same activity as one another. To put this matter the other way round, where the use of the home is restricted to family, the likelihood of other relationships being limited, and being conceived of as limited, to particular social settings is increased. However, while being a most important element in the overall picture, the idea of the home being thought of as private does not account fully for the limitation of sociable relationships. The context a relationship is defined as relevant to can be widened without the home being used as a centre for interaction. Instead these two elements – the home as private and relationships being limited – should be seen as feeding off one another and being interdependent rather than as cause and effect, for each reinforces the other conceptually and organisationally.

From what has been written it can be seen that middle- and working-class non-kin sociability involves distinct patterns. Further, although conclusive evidence is lacking because of the analytical procedures used in previous studies, there is a good deal of indirect support for the thesis that working-class sociable relationships, unlike middle-class ones, tend to be defined by particular contexts and settings. Many facts of working-class culture reported in these earlier studies are compatible with this interpretation. I want to conclude this chapter by adding a few more pieces to this cultural jigsaw. Whilst these are not concerned with sociability as such, they add weight to the material already presented by pointing to differences in middle- and working-class life that help generate and support different assumptions about the way non-kin relationships are routinely organised.

We can begin by returning to the issue of the use the home plays in non-kin sociability. As noted, entertaining in the home is a key way by which the middle class are able to transcend particular structures and situations. Conversely, not using the home for entertaining non-kin makes it more likely, but by no means inevitable, that the working-class respondents' relationships will remain bound to a given setting. A partial explanation of this divergence lies in the different material circumstances of members of the two groups. Not only is entertaining at home potentially expensive, but it sets in motion a series of transactions which need to be reciprocated and which are harder to escape from than is the case with more structured relationships. More than this, admitting someone into the home is in a sense to admit them to one's 'back-region' (Goffman, 1959) and entails revealing one's 'self' in a way not entailed in other settings. To the extent that material possessions are used to judge worth, or perhaps more important are believed to be used by others to judge worth, then the supposed costs to self-esteem are potentially greater the more modest are the material circumstances. The middle-class person has less to lose as what he or she reveals is likely to be taken as reflecting successful achievement. In addition, the facilities of the middle-class home are likely to be more conducive to the creation of the ambience required for relaxed interaction.

In passages referred to earlier, Lupton and Mitchell (1954) and Young and Willmott (1962) both suggest that working-class sociable relationships are limited to something less than friendship in order that the demands others make of a person can be controlled. Restricting access to the home is one element in this as it increases the control a person has over what is revealed in relationships. But over and above this, restricting relationships to particular contexts and activities in general limits the demands others can make of you and you of them. Each area of life is segmented and, in a sense, protected from other areas. In any one, other aspects of self are held to be private. In this way an individual with more limited resources can restrict his obligations to others. Indeed, provided they are not made apparent in the setting in hand, the question of his limited resources need never become an issue. An extension of this is Oxley's contention that restricting the rules of relevance of relationships to particular contexts and topics emphasises the equality between the interactants by making potentially disruptive disparities in other areas irrelevant (Oxley, 1974). The middle class, because of their superior material circumstances, need be less concerned with protecting self in this way, and can consequently emphasise individuality rather than egalitarianism.

Thus the way of organising non-kin sociable relationships discussed in this chapter gives the working class greater control over the demands that can be made of them and their degree of commitment to a relationship. Distinct middle- and working-class patterns can be maintained because they are rarely questioned. The rules of relevance applied can be taken for granted and treated as normal because the other people party to the relationship also take this form as the natural way of ordering relationships. This is ensured by the class homophily in friendship. As numerous studies have shown, few sociable relationships of any importance to those involved cross class boundaries (Lazarsfeld and Merton, 1954; Williams, 1956; Stacey, 1960; Littlejohn, 1963; Klein, 1965; Goldthorpe et al., 1969; Hill, 1976). That members of the two classes organise relationships differently not only depends on this, but also in its way makes the development of cross-class relationships less likely because the conflict over the appropriate rules of relevance will be apparent to both sides early on. Where two people take different things as natural, each is likely to regard the other's performance as to some extent artificial.

But while assumed orderings of one's world, including one's sociable relationships, are supported and legitimated through being shared by others, there is another factor that is important to the process. Following Sapir and Whorf, we would expect the language people use to reflect the way they order the world and to support the constructions they create. In this light the parallels between Basil Bernstein's conceptions of 'restricted' and 'elaborated' linguistic codes and the patterns of friendship described in this and the previous chapter are of special significance. These parallels are evident in much of Bernstein's work but are put most succinctly in a passage in 'A sociolinguistic approach to socialisation: with some reference to educability'. Bernstein writes (1973, pp. 170–1; emphasis in original):

'In terms of what is transmitted verbally, an elaborated code encourages the speaker to focus upon the experience of others, as different from his own. In the case of a restricted code, what is transmitted verbally usually refers to the other person in terms of a common group or status membership. What is said here epitomizes the social structure and its basis of shared assumptions. Thus restricted codes could be considered status or positional codes whereas elaborated codes are orientated to persons. An elaborated code, in principle, presupposes a sharp boundary or gap between self and others which is crossed through the creation of speech which specifically fits a differentiated 'other'. In this sense, an elaborated code is oriented towards a person rather than a social category or status. In the case of a restricted code, the boundary or gap is between sharers and non-sharers of the code. In this sense a restricted code is positional or status *not* person oriented. It presupposes a generalized rather than a differentiated other.'

These ideas of Bernstein's fit in well with the class-based differences in non-kin sociable relationships specified above. Both emphasise the importance of received social structures in working-class members' conceptions and orderings of the world, as against the more individual-oriented conceptions of middle-class members.

An important point to remember here is that language is not

merely a means of expressing reality but itself shapes and structures the way reality is viewed. As Bernstein continually points out, the two factors of linguistic code and the organisation of social relations are interdependent, each one supporting the other. That is, the manner in which relationships are expressed reflects as well as structures those relationships. The two processes are interwoven. 'According to [the view taken here], the form of the social relation or, more generally, the social structure generates distinct linguistic forms or codes and *these codes essentially transmit the culture and so constrain behaviour.*' 'The general socio-linguistic thesis attempts to explore how symbolic systems are both realizations and regulators of the structure of social relationships' (Bernstein, 1973, pp. 143 and 194; emphasis in original). With respect to the present research it can be seen that if this is true the language that people use is itself a phenomenon that helps maintain the assumption that a particular way of ordering relationships is natural. It is extremely interesting that the interpretation of sociable relationships developed above receives corroborative support from a source as discrete as Bernstein's work.

Chapter 7

Sociability with Kin

As already suggested in Chapter 4, kin are a category of people defined by comparatively explicit rules, based on a combination of biological and legal concepts, namely, ties through blood and marriage. By applying these rules, genealogies can be extended in depth and width indefinitely. In practical terms, one problem is knowing when to stop. As Rosser and Harris have pointed out: 'If one had time enough to spend on this exercise, it would be possible to sit down with an informant, better still with a household group, particularly if this contains an elderly woman, and record the family tree thoroughly section by section to its farthest limits, in the memory of the informant or household group, including remote relatives through marriages' (1965, p. 196).

Like these authors, we can question the utility of this exercise for sociological purposes, especially in an analysis of sociable behaviour. As many studies have shown that secondary kin are of comparatively little significance in most people's lives (Firth, 1956; Rosser and Harris, 1965; Adams, 1968; Firth *et al.*, 1970), the predominant concern in this chapter will be the sociable relationships existing between adult primary kin, i.e. parents, siblings and (adult) children.

There is a good deal of variety in the way different people organise and define these relationships. While, conventionally, nearly everyone expresses emotional concern and attachment for his or her kin, this is quite clearly not synonymous with sociable involvement. For some people primary kin provide major figures in their sociable landscapes but for others they are far less important. The aim of this chapter will be to analyse the underlying similarities and variations in the rules of relevance applied by different groups of people to these relationships. In doing this I shall emphasise the importance of viewing kinship as a social network rather than as a series of discrete relationships, and shall concentrate more heavily than is usual on sibling relationships. When contrasted with those discussed in the previous two chapters, sibling relationships exemplify most aptly important differences in the organisation of kin and non-kin relationships.

KIN RELATIONSHIPS

Whether or not the Western kinship system is structurally isolated in comparison to other kinship systems, the fondly held dogma that the nuclear family is *socially* isolated has been well and truly laid to rest (see Harris, 1969). In the main this has been achieved by demonstrating the continuing significance of the parent–adult-child bond after the latter's maturation. Certainly this relationship has been analysed more comprehensively in recent studies than any other kin relationship. Starting with the work of the Institute of Community Studies in England and Sussman's research in the United States, the nature and importance of the exchange of services and aid flowing between the two generations has been well documented in many research studies. In Britain, Young and Willmott's outstanding description of the mother–daughter bond in Bethnal Green has been added to and amended by their own later research (1967, 1973), and by that of such people as Rosser and Harris (1961, 1965), Gavron (1966) and Barker (1972). While his study has not been replicated to anything like the same extent, Bell's analysis of the importance of the continuing flow of material aid from father to son in socially immobile middle-class families during the early phases of the son's family-cycle is as illuminating and sociologically significant as Young and Willmott's work (Bell, 1968a, 1968b, 1972).

Thus, far from being insignificant, kin relationships have been shown to be of great consequence to the smooth functioning of normal life. There is a general acceptance of Litwak's model of the modified extended family, a model which highlights the interdependence of bureaucracies in modern society with non-bureaucratic primary groups, especially kin-based ones (Litwak, 1960a; 1960b; 1965). Bureaucracies have not taken over the functions of the wider family; rather these functions are shared. As Harris notes, 'the distinction between what the former can do and what the latter can do does not depend on the type of activity (political, religious, economic, etc.) but upon the extent to which the activity is sufficiently patterned, repetitive and predictable in its occurrence, and the extent to which the need for it is easily recognizable' (1969, pp. 106–7).

Thus in Western society the nuclear family is not socially isolated, nor is kinship reduced to some mythical 'pure' form, 'uncontaminated by any instrumental considerations' (see Morgan, 1975, p. 78). Certainly kinship is expressive but it is not *only* expressive. Consequently there must be reservations in accepting claims such as Reiss's that the 'function of these extended kinship relationships appears to be basically those performed by primary friendship relationships; personality satisfaction including a sense of belonging, companionship and security' (quoted in Morgan, 1975, p. 78). Especially for parent–adult-child ties, the alternative here of course is not the straightforward reverse of this, i.e. that they do not perform these functions for each other, but that instrumental and expressive factors reinforce and complement each other. This point has been developed by Barker (1972). She shows how the parents of newly married couples encourage continued interaction and the expression of affection and obligation through the provision of varied material services. Whilst this process is not seen by many as a direct form of exchange, Barker is undoubtedly correct in claiming it functions in this way. Naturally the basis of exchange between parents and adult children changes throughout the life-cycle, depending on each side's circumstances, but its importance remains. As far as the present context is concerned, this exchange nexus helps sustain the conventional prescriptions which shape their sociable relationship and, *contra* Reiss, differentiates it from (non-kin) ties of friendship.

PARENT–ADULT-CHILD SOCIABILITY

What appears to be the most banal feature of parent–adult-child relationships is in fact the most significant: *in one form or another these relationships persist.* Notwithstanding the difficulty of interpreting them, a major corollary of the tables of contact rates produced in many studies is that where parents are alive the enormous majority of these relationships are extant. It is most unusual for them to lapse. As Adams writes: 'Even when affectional ties are weak, general obligation results in the maintenance of regular contact with parents by whatever means are available' (1971, p. 127). Firth et al. add to this by noting that even when the relationship between a parent and an adult child is soured, 'the strains are apt to be endured at a much greater intensity or for a much longer time than in the case of other kin before a breach occurs' (1970, p. 401). The three cases (out of 168) they report of these relationships breaking down completely followed acrimonious divorces by the parents in which one parent was sided with against the other. So, too, in the Selden Hey research only one respondent – who described himself as 'the black sheep' of the family – was no longer in contact with a still-living parent.

The range of relationships that exist between parents and their adult children is wide, as numerous kinship studies have testified (Rosser and Harris, 1965; Bell, 1968b; Firth et al., 1970). However, while not all of them are amiable at all times, the great majority appear to be based on broadly similar rules of relevance once class and gender differences are taken into account. The details of interaction – its frequency, its duration, the specific exchanges involved – depend upon a variety of factors, including geographical location and the present stage in family- and life-cycles, but basic patterns appear to underly the way these relationships are usually defined. At a minimum the rules of relevance generally applied in these relationships are characterised by what Adams (1967) calls 'positive concern'. Regular interaction occurs, usually in the form of visits of differing lengths, so that contact between the generations is maintained. And maintaining contact is a main end in itself. The aim is to ensure that both sides have a general knowledge of each other's well-being and hear one another's news. While there is a strong element of obligation, the visits may well be experienced as quite enjoyable. However, it is important, to note that enjoyment is not their direct purpose, as it is, for example, with interaction between friends. Indeed, interaction is not considered 'social' in the same sense that interaction with friends is. The visits are simply a way of expressing concern and interest. To this extent the rules of relevance applied to the relationships are at the same time both general and restricted. The activities engaged in tend to be limited to ones which take place in each other's home, and many aspects of life are considered inappropriate to, and outside, the realm of these relationships. None the less it is recognised that the generations have a right to an interest in each other and a genuine concern for one another's well-being.

An example from the Selden Hey research will serve as an illustration, though many previous studies also include relevant material. (See, for example, Young and Willmott, 1962; Adams, 1965; Firth et al., 1970.) In particular this shows how infrequent, regular visits provide a vehicle that allow a continuing but limited form of involvement.

Mr Giddings's parents lived in Southend and were seen, mainly in Southend, every five or six weeks. The Giddingses usually went down there for the day. Although their visits had become less taxing as their children got older, the Giddingses gave the strong impression that the visits were not enjoyed as sociable occasions. It was quite evident that Mr Giddings's parents were not involved at a day-to-day level with their son's life, and would not have been even if they lived near. For example, Mrs Giddings pointed out that her husband's parents never rang up just to say 'hello'. They would always have some explicit purpose. Similarly Mr Giddings did not confide in his parents over personal matters. Over major decisions their advice might be asked, or at least plans discussed with them, not necessarily because their opinion would be influential in any decisions made but because it was felt that generally parents had a right to be kept informed of any major undertakings that affected their offspring's personal or familial situation. Thus, the rules of relevance they had constructed for the relationship were based on an underlying recognition of the right and duty of at least some limited form of involvement. Similarly it was recognised that practical help could be expected from Mr Giddingses' parents in circumstances of need. For example, when the Giddingses' younger son was in hospital, Mr Giddings's father offered them his car so that they could visit him more easily.

As well as illustrating the basis of much parent–adult-child inter-action, this example shows that aid can be given in one form or another even where sociable involvement as such is defined by the participants as limited. Indeed the knowledge that these kin can be depended upon for material and non-material aid where feasible in times of need is an important element in the relationship. It represents a further aspect of the overall positive concern shown by the generations for each other. As discussed earlier, it both expresses this concern and encourages it by the setting up of obligations.

The evidence from previous research would suggest that the relationship males have with their parents follows the broad patterns outlined here. For example Young and Willmott were 'struck time and again by the regularity with which men kept in touch with their parents . . . "I make it my business to call round to see my mother every Sunday" said Mr Wilkins. 'I never miss a week." Another husband suggested the triumph of duty over inclination when he said, "I usually go round on a Sunday morning. You can't ignore them – they only live round the corner" ' (1962, pp. 73–4). Firth et al. similarly point to positive yet limited concern: 'But what is particularly significant in the social relations of parents to married children is the way in which superficial harmony covers a range of disparate attitudes. Common in our material was the expression on the part of married son or daughter that relations with a parent were friendly but superficial; that he or she liked the parent but did not feel they could discuss intimate matters with him or her' (1970, pp. 404–5).

Distance, of course, affects the frequency and duration of inter-action. Middle-class sons tend to be geographically mobile and con-sequently visit their parents at weekends or during holiday periods, maintaining contact by phone or letter in the meantime (Bell, 1968b; Firth et al., 1970). As their parents are more likely to live close at hand, working-class males tend more to visit their parents for shorter if more frequent periods. Some indeed appear to do so at a regular time each week (see Young and Willmott, 1962, pp. 73–5). However, these differences are less significant than the similarities in the underlying rules of relevance applied to the relationships.

Overall, though there is variation in this, female respondents in most kinship studies appear to be more involved, both sociably and emotionally, with their parents than are male respondents. There are, however, important differences between the two classes in its extent. While Bell emphasises the structural importance of the son–father bond in the giving of aid, studies concentrating more directly on sociability suggest that middle-class female respondents tend to be slightly more involved with their parents both in their frequency of interaction and in the terms they use to describe their relationships. For example, in the Selden Hey research the middle-class females tended to express affection more readily and were more likely to define their relationships with their parents as being closer than their husbands' with theirs. However, even though parents might be seen regularly and not infrequently, these relationships, like their male equivalents, do not appear to be defined as 'social', nor explicitly undertaken for enjoyment's sake. From the evidence available in previous studies – and once more this is normally not presented in a form fully appropriate for our purposes – it would seem these relationships are removed from non-domestic, non-familial spheres of activity and seen as somewhat peripheral to the overall organisation of these people's sociable lives. In the Selden Hey research, none of the middle-class female respondents referred to their parents as 'friends' or appeared to think of them in this way. Consequently the main strand of these relationships is still captured by Adam's phrase 'positive concern'. As with their husbands, the expression of general interest and concern, and a concomitant flow and exchange of material and non-material aid, are the most important features in the definitions held of these relationships. A further point worth making here is that although middle-class female respondents normally seem to be a little more involved sociably with their mothers than their fathers, partly no doubt because of their occupying similar positions within the household, the difference in their relationships with their two parents is not as marked as it typically is for working-class females.

To illustrate these arguments I shall again draw on the Selden Hey material. As Mr Giddings's relationship with his parents was presented earlier, it will be appropriate to discuss Mrs Giddings's with hers now, the more so as this material aptly portrays the points I am making here.

Mrs Giddings's parents moved to Selden Hey a year after the Giddingses had. While it was implicitly recognised that a major motive behind the move was to be near their daughter and grandchildren, the two couples had never discussed the reasons overtly. ('It would have been too embarrassing for both of us.') Considering their proximity, Mrs Giddings does not interact a great deal with her parents. Her father, who works in the meat trade in London, usually brings a joint of meat round for them on Friday evenings, but is otherwise seen rarely. Despite her husband being away a good deal because of his work, Mrs Giddings only sees her mother once or twice a week, usually over a cup of coffee. On the other hand, her children spend a good deal of time at their grandparents, frequently going round to play and have tea after school. It was to this that Mrs Giddings was largely referring when she said 'It pays us in many ways to have them near'. Apart from larger family ceremonies they only interact in their respective houses, and Mrs Giddings is conscious of excluding parts of her world from her parents. Like her husband's relationship to his parents. Mrs Giddings's relationship to her parents is based on a recognition by both sides that each is interested in and concerned about the other but that this concern and interest does not imply that interaction need be extensive, nor that the implicit rules of relevance that govern the relationship need to be wide-ranging. Thus while interaction is more frequent with her parents than her husband's, her parents do not figure prominently in her social life. Their relationship is however influenced by the larger part her parents play in their grandchildren's lives.

While it would appear that working-class females' relationships with their fathers are similar to those discussed above, their relationships with their mothers tend to be somewhat different. With their fathers, the expression of positive concern is again paramount, once more being manifested in the main through occasional visits and a continued knowledge of one another's circumstances. The mother–daughter relationship, which of course following Young and Willmott's seminal monograph is the most researched of all, seems generally to be based on a far greater degree of involvement. Naturally there are variations in this, but on the whole their mothers tend to play a more prominent part in their daughter's routine, day-to-day life and, important to note, are expected to do so. Such greater involvement is taken for granted and regarded as the natural way of ordering these relationships. While the pattern described by Young and Willmott as typical for Bethnal Green would now appear to be an extreme version of this rather than the norm, Townsend's remark that this borough is not 'a sub-cultural island where strange customs have been magically preserved' (1963, p. 236) is certainly pertinent. The pattern Young and Willmott found is not totally dissimilar in its essence to that described by Rosser and Harris for Swansea. Indeed these authors write: 'It seems sufficient to say that the vivid descriptions of Young and Willmott of the close and enduring tie, expressed both in terms of practical domestic organisation and in emotional responses, between mother and married daughter in Bethnal Green could easily have been written about Swansea' 1965, p. 227).

Essentially working-class females are likely to include their mothers in their routine activities. They define them as more central to the organisation of their social life, and are more willing to confide in them and discuss problems. As would be expected, most of their joint activities are centred on their homes and domestic duties. This is facilitated by the relatively high geographical stability of the generations. In the Selden Hey research, there tended to be a good deal of 'popping in' (as distinct from 'visiting') between working-class mothers and daughters, but even where interaction was no more frequent than it was for the middle-class females, the way the relationship was described assumed that mothers had a greater right to be involved in a large part of their life. In other words different normative assumptions were being made about the 'normal' or 'natural' state of mother–daughter relationships. Unlike the others, these respondents were more likely to define their inter-action as 'social' and regard and treat their mothers as equivalent to 'friends'. The difference between working-class mother–daughter relationships and other parent–adult-child ones is illustrated by one of the Selden Hey respondent's relationships with her two married children. Her son, like those in Young and Willmott's study (1962, pp. 73–5), visited her regularly each Friday evening. ('That's the only time you can't come round.') Her daughter, on the other hand, though living in the same town as her brother, 'popped round' far more frequently, three or four times a week 'just for a cup of tea and a chat'. In addition, it was clear from her remarks that this respondent was involved in a wider range of activities with her daughter than with her son and knew a good deal more about her everyday experiences.

RELATIONSHIPS WITH SIBLINGS

In this section I shall discuss the sociable relationships of brothers and sisters. Whilst they have been somewhat neglected in the litera-ture compared to parental relationships, sibling relationships none the less appear to illustrate many of the most important features of kinship in our society. In particular they demonstrate clearly both the 'choice' element of the British kinship system (see Firth, 1956), and that most kin relationships cannot be understood in isolation from one another but only when seen as part of a kin network. In this section I shall do as I have done before and provide necessarily short accounts of two of the Selden Hey respondents' sibling relationships to provide a backcloth for the arguments that follow.

Susan Barnes, aged 23, is married to a junior manager in a national company selling confectionery. She has four siblings, two brothers and a sister older than herself and a younger brother. Her parents and her siblings all live in south-west England.

Geoffrey, who is four years older than Mrs Barnes, is married and lives in Weston-super-Mare. The only time Geoffrey and Mrs Barnes meet is when the Barneses are visiting Mrs Barnes's parents in Bristol. Geoffrey and his wife go to his parents' on Sundays for Sunday lunch, so would be seen then. Because they meet this way, the Barneses would be unlikely to go to the trouble of visiting Geoffrey at his house when they are staying with Mrs Barnes's parents. They also thought it unlikely, though possible, that Geoffrey would ever come to visit them in Selden Hey. One reason given for this was that the Barneses did not know Geoffrey's wife very well.

Terry, who is two years older than Mrs Barnes, is married and lives in Bristol. When they were younger Mrs Barnes and Terry did not get along with each other particularly well. According to Mrs Barnes, Terry and Margaret used to gang up against her and Nigel. However, since Terry got married, they interact sociably with one another a good deal. The reason for this is that Mrs Barnes and Terry's wife, Cheryl, have become very close friends and get along with each other extremely well. So, for example, whenever they go to stay with Mrs Barnes's parents they make an effort to see Terry and Cheryl and are likely to go out with them. Similarly they expect Terry and Cheryl to visit them in Selden Hey.

Margaret, one year older than Mrs Barnes, is single and recently spent a good deal of time abroad in Europe and North America. As with Terry, in childhood there was a good deal of conflict and tension between Margaret and Mrs Barnes, made worse by their having to share a bedroom. As teenagers they were always arguing with one another, and never went out or did things together. Since then their relationship has become less tempestuous, but Mrs Barnes does not regard Margaret as a friend in the way she does Cheryl and still has few interests in common with her. When Margaret returns from North America she will probably visit the Barneses in Selden Hey for a week or so, but apart from this is likely to be seen only when both are at their parents' home.

Nigel, aged 19, is single and lives with his parents. Mrs Barnes had been closest to Nigel throughout her childhood, and both she and her husband thought this was still the case. His interests and ideas corresponded far more with Mrs Barnes's than those of any of her other siblings. As he lived at home he was seen a good deal when the Barneses visited Mrs Barnes's parents, and whenever the latter visited Selden Hey Nigel always came too. It seemed highly likely that when Nigel left home, their interaction would be similar to that between the Barneses and Cheryl and Terry, the more so as Mr Barnes said he too got on better with Nigel than any of the others.

Mr Knowles, aged 50, is a factory hand in a large manufacturing plant some distance from Selden Hey. He has eight siblings, four brothers and four sisters.

Ray is eleven years older than Mr Knowles and lives with his wife Dora in a town near Selden Hey. Mr and Mrs Knowles, Ray and Dora and Peter and Betty (see below) go to a social club together every fortnight. While there, the six of them form a recognised group, sitting and talking with one another. However, the Knowleses appear to see little of Ray and Dora apart from these regular evenings at the club. Mrs Knowles said she got on very well with Dora in this social setting but was not close to her outside it. She did not confide in her or regard her as a friend in the way she did Betty.

Alan is nine years older than Mr Knowles and with his wife runs a pub in a village some 15 miles from Selden Hey. Every couple of months, Mr and Mrs Knowles and Peter and Betty go there for a combination of visit and social evening out. Alan and his wife never visit the Knowleses or go out elsewhere with them.

Helen is eight years older than Mr Knowles and lives in the same town as Ray. The Knowleses' interaction with her and her husband is limited to the occasional visits they make to Helen's home. They never go out with them, nor do Helen and her husband visit them in Selden Hey.

Irene is five years older than Mr Knowles and lives with her husband and Mr Knowles's mother in the same town as Ray and Helen. As with Helen, interaction with Irene is limited to visits to her home. These are more frequent with Irene because Mr Knowles goes primarily to visit his mother. The impression is that if his mother did not live with her, Irene would not be seen any more than Helen. As it is, Mr Knowles hears of his other siblings through his mother (and Irene) as they too all regularly visit their mother. Occasionally, either by chance or by arrangement, he meets one or other of his siblings on these visits.

Denise is Irene's twin sister and lives in London. She is normally seen when she comes to stay at Irene's. Very occasionally the Knowleses visit her home but they would not do so merely because they happened to be in London.

Peter is three years older than Mr Knowles and lives in a village 5 miles from Selden Hey. He is in effect Mr Knowles's closest friend, and his wife Betty is one of Mrs Knowles's two best friends (the other being a sister-in-law, her brother's wife). They see each other regularly each weekend. On Saturdays they usually go to the club (with Ray and Dora) or for a meal or to a dance together, and on Sundays always have tea together and play cards in the evening. Invariably the two couples go on holiday together as well.

Philip is two years younger than Mr Knowles and lives in Cambridge. Unlike Denise, he and his wife visit the Knowleses every few months and are likely to be seen when Philip and his family visit his mother at Irene's. The Knowleses also occasionally make trips to Cambridge to visit Philip and his family.

Penny is five years younger than Mr Knowles and lives in the midlands. Because her husband travels abroad quite frequently on business trips, Penny often comes and stays with Irene. When she does the Knowleses make sure they see her, and occasionally go and stay with her and her family for weekends.

These examples illustrate the major features of the way sibling relationships are typically organised. The first factor to note is that, as with parents, sibling relationships endure. Previous research clearly indicates that the majority of people interact directly with their siblings. In addition, where there is no face-to-face interaction, phone calls and letters provide means by which contact and knowledge can be mantained. Firth *et al.*, for example, report that their respondents were in contact with 94 per cent of their siblings. They write: 'complete lapse or severance of social ties with grown-up siblings was very rare; the bond of membership in the same natal family implied the maintenance of *some* form of social relationship' (1970, p. 429; their emphasis). Apart from Townsend, who concentrates on the weakening of sibling relationships in old age (1963), other writers, while not providing exact figures, imply clearly that maintaining contact is the norm for siblings. Similarly in the Selden Hey research all but one respondent were in contact with all their living siblings.

The endurance of sibling relationships may not seem remarkable in itself, but is of great interest when a comparison is made with the forms of non-kin relationships discussed in the previous chapters. It supports Schneider's view that in Western society ties of blood are taken as being more durable than relationships based on other criteria. Normative convention makes the severing of social relationships with siblings more problematic than the severing of relationships with people known through other circumstances. Neighbours or other non-kin associates may be quietly shed but it is less appropriate to drop a sibling in the same way. As noted in Chapter 4, blood ties cannot be rescinded; their continued existence is taken to be synonymous with the continued existence of a social relationship between the siblings. One can have an ex-friend and an ex-workmate but not an ex-sibling.

The second fact about sibling relationships worth noting is that, despite their range and variety, the majority of them appear to be based on broadly similar principles. On the whole the rules of relevance governing the sorts of activity and types of setting appropriate to them have basic elements in common. Put simply, the emphasis in these rules, as with the relationships discussed in the previous section, is merely on maintaining contact for its own sake. Siblings wish to keep in touch with each other and know in a general way what the other's overall situation is. Thus Young and Willmott point out that siblings usually keep in touch with each other whether or not their parents are alive (1962, ch. 5). Firth and his associates state that 93 per cent of their middle-class respondents' sibling relationships could be described as 'positive' or 'indifferent'. In a positive relationship, 'no great enthusiasm may be expressed but the maintenance of contact is regarded as normal' (1970, p. 430). 'Indifferent' means that 'no active dislike is expressed [and] some contact is maintained' (1970, p. 430). On the basis of his American data, Adams writes: 'Adult sibling relations may be best characterized by the terms *interest* and *comparison*. The term "interest" signifies less of the positive, active element of concern than was apparent in relations with parents . . . Nevertheless, fairly frequent contact is maintained, demonstrating the interest which siblings ordinarily have in how the other is getting along' (1971, p. 127). In a later summary of recent research, Adams further wrote: 'There is a basic interest on the part of siblings in each other's activities and achievements or failures, but in only a few cases does the relation become one of close friendship in adulthood (though this occurs more frequently in the working class)' (1970, p. 583).

The rather limited involvement signified in the above quotations is generally achieved through siblings interacting with one another occasionally, supplemented by letters and telephone calls where applicable and news learnt through the network of other family members. Because maintaining a diffuse, limited involvement with one another is seen as the main focus of sibling relationships, the range of activities that the majority of siblings engage in with one another tends to be modest. For most siblings they are restricted to visits to each other's home or, for the younger respondents, meetings at their parents' home: the point being that this is all that is necessary to maintain the required contact. The way the relationships are defined means there is no need to interact in other situations or settings, including those, like pubs or clubs, which are 'social' in the general meaning of this term. The majority of these relationships do not require extrinsically enjoyable activities or settings, for extraneous enjoyment does not enter into the definitions held of them. To chat with one another and be sociable during visits is all that is necessary to maintain and express solidarity. Interaction may in fact be enjoyed, but looking for extrinsic enjoyment through other activities is not seen as relevant to most of them. In this they are clearly different from the non-kin sociable relationships discussed in the previous chapter.

The examples given at the beginning of this section illustrate the predominance of this way of defining sibling relationships. Despite their many differences, the relationships between Mr Knowles and the majority of his siblings and Mrs Barnes and Geoff and Margaret (and to a lesser extent Nigel) all basically reflect this pattern of limited but continuing involvement based on occasional interaction in a domestic setting combined with news and information of one another learnt from a variety of sources.

As cultural traits develop within particular social structures, it is important to ascertain the features of kinship structure that shape the rules of relevance of sibling relationships. In particular, why is is that the majority of sibling relationships are based on the principles outlined above? The most important aspect of kinship structure pertinent here is the fact that kinship forms a social network. The biologically and legally ordered genealogy is transformed into a network of *social* relationships, each of which can constrain and structure other relationships. Considering the effect other relationships have helps explain why the majority of sibling relationships take the form they do.

Sibling relationships are affected by other relationships in the kin network in a variety of ways. To begin with, intermediary kin provide a most important source of knowledge about siblings not interacted with directly. Whilst other siblings may play a part, parents, and especially mothers, are particularly important in this for they frequently provide a form of brokerage service for their children as a result of their central position in the elementary family network. News and gossip of other kin is an important topic in most kin interaction. Consequently there is almost always some flow of information about other siblings during interaction between any two of them and perhaps more routinely during interaction between the parents and each of the siblings. This flow of information serves as a means both of expressing and of reinforcing the sibling solidarity implicit in the kinship ideology.

Parents and to a lesser extent other siblings may also encourage direct interaction. For example, as with Mrs Barnes above, parents may arrange for siblings to be at the parents' home at the same time. Conversely, where all the parties live relatively close to one another, siblings may meet by chance rather than arrangement if they happen to visit their parents simultaneously. Young and Willmott give copious examples to support their contention that 'both sons and daughters see their mother *(and each other)* at her home more than anywhere else' (1962, p. 77; emphasis added). Less directly, Townsend (in contrast to Cumming and Schneider, 1961) discusses how sibling relationships are weakened by the death of parents (1963). Similarly Adams writes: 'Ageing parents play a particularly central role . . . in perpetuating their nuclear families of procreation, i.e. in linking siblings together after they leave the parental home' (1971, p. 130).

In such cases the parental home may serve, in effect, as an informal centre for the dispersed elementary family, facilitating interaction and the distribution of news. The emphasis here is on *facilitating*, for usually interaction occurs and news is learnt of siblings whether parents are alive or not; the parental home merely provides a convenient locale. Again the Bethnal Green studies illustrate this. Both Young and Willmott (1962) and Townsend (1963) show that while the amount of interaction decreases with the deaths of their parents, siblings in general continue to maintain contact. 'So the siblings usually keep in touch with each other after the mother's death. If they live at a distance from each other and do not meet often, they still communicate with each other. They send Christmas and birthday cards, and keep the family news flowing' (Young and Willmott, 1962, p. 81). Occasionally parents may exert some moral pressure on their children to ensure they interact. In most cases, though, there is little need for much parental pressure, the parents' main function being to promote interaction by providing convenient opportunities for their children to meet one another.

Because the kinship network is operative, geographical dispersion is a more significant variable in sibling relationships than geographical separation alone, even though the latter affects the frequency and length of interaction. Quite frequently some siblings live in one location, usually that of the parental home, while others have moved away. These latter often stay with their parents or a particular sibling for some period and meet their (other) siblings during this time. This was the case, for example, with Mr Knowles's sister Penny and with Mrs Barnes. Because of their greater geographical mobility this factor affects the middle class most.

Stated baldly, these features of kinship being a network of relationships appear self-evident. Their importance is that they all structure sibling relationships in a manner that helps sustain the cultural assumptions made about the nature of such close blood ties. In other words, the various network factors described above enable sibling relationships to endure despite the comparatively limited exchange content involved in most of them. While other factors – such as affection and the experiences of shared childhood – are also clearly important, any explanation of why sibling relationships persist when non-kin relationships with higher exchange contents tend not to must include reference to the structuring imposed by the kinship network.

VARIATIONS IN SIBLING RELATIONSHIPS

While the majority of sibling relationships are based on similar rules of relevance, there is none the less variation in the nature of the interaction that occurs between different siblings, including those of the same individual. Firth and his associates have discussed such differences with regard to their middle-class respondents in some detail and have shown that a variety of situational and structural contingencies act here. Some, such as geographical dispersion and parental influence, have already been discussed. Others are also important. For example, it is not only when siblings live some distance apart from each other that geographical location affects the nature of their interaction. As Young and Willmott (1962) show, where siblings live in close proximity to one another, they tend to deviate from the usual pattern of sibling-visiting. Because they quite frequently meet each other by chance in passing (as well as at their parents' perhaps) there is less need to visit one another. They can maintain contact with one another through these unplanned casual meetings, and do not need to express their solidarity by purposeful visits to each other's homes. A similar pattern was found with some of the working-class Selden Hey respondents. It was most marked in the case of Mr Clegg, seven of whose thirteen siblings lived in Selden Hey. Five of these seven neither visited the Cleggs nor were visited by them. Instead they relied on their casual and haphazard chance meetings to hear each other's news.

A large age difference between siblings can also affect their relationship. As Firth *et al.* write: 'Siblings separated by a great age gap tended to regard each other with much less social interest than those close together in age' (1970, p. 432). Young and Willmott also imply that such siblings may be less close to each other, noting that there may be as much as twenty years separating siblings, though clearly this is less likely with current demographic tendencies than previously. Where it occurs it means that while one sibling was growing up, the other had left the parental home and was starting his own family of marriage, so that there was less interaction than was usual between siblings. One of the Selden Hey respondents, whose brother was seventeen years older than him, jokingly remarked: 'I never knew I had a brother till I was fifteen and started to work with him.'

Less extreme differences in the stages siblings have reached in their life-cycle can also affect interaction. If one sibling is at the child-rearing stage but another is not, their different situations may make interaction less likely. Indeed when both siblings are married with families, meetings can often be more difficult to arrange than when children are not involved, especially where the siblings live some distance apart. Old age may also reduce sibling interaction, especially if one or both siblings is infirm, and when they live some distance apart. Travelling becomes more arduous, as does the effort needed to entertain. Townsend has discussed the variety of factors that weaken sibling relationships amongst the elderly at great length (1963). However, contrary to this, on the basis of their American data, Cumming and Schneider (1961) argue that sibling solidarity is particularly prominent with people in the final stages of the family life-cycle as to some extent at this time sibling bonds appear to replace ties with their now-adult children.

There is also some disagreement in the research literature on the effect on sibling relationships of social mobility. This corresponds with the rather divergent findings that have been reported on the effects of social mobility on wider kin relationships (see Schneider and Homans, 1955; Litwak, 1960a; Adams, 1965; Bell, 1968b). Townsend writes: 'Sometimes differences in social class appeared to have caused siblings to lose touch . . . One or two said they would not dream of seeking help from high-status siblings even when ill' (1962, p. 118). In part Townsend, like Adams (1968), sees sibling competition as the reason for this. 'Siblings share childhood together. There is a natural equality, but also a basis for competition, between them. If one achieves more than the others in adult life the competitiveness is likely to be stressed' (1963, p. 118). Firth et al., while recognising that differences in the siblings' income level may, in economic matters, result in some embarrassment, deny that social mobility is 'responsible to any significant extent for coolness between siblings' (1970, p. 432). This disagreement may well be a consequence of Townsend's respondents being relatively poor and Firth et al.'s notably successful.

However, while all the above factors can affect the interaction between siblings, by far the most important consideration is their compatibility and liking for one another. As was illustrated by Mrs Barnes's relationships, this can vary a good deal, though the variation is less in adult life than in childhood and adolescence. Firth et al., claim that sibling jealously and rivalry originating at an early age is one of 'the two most important factors . . . involved in the more severe breaches of sibling relationships' (1970, p. 432). They none the less provide a number of illustrations (e.g. pp. 427, 433–4) that suggest that sibling rivalry, and the tension and hostility that goes with it, is normally dissipated as the siblings get older. Certainly this appeared to be the case in the Selden Hey research. A number of respondents reported that they squabbled and bickered with particular siblings in childhood but now felt far less aggressive towards them. These siblings might not particularly enjoy interacting with one another in any positive way but nevertheless they do interact, and can apparently manage to do so without too much tension arising.

There appear to be two factors that militate against lack of compatibility or disliking drastically affecting sibling relationships. First there is what I have termed the network effect. As noted, parents especially can be influential in arranging for siblings to interact. The second factor is the limited form of interaction required in most sibling relationships. Because at its minimum this involves little more than chatting and being friendly on occasion, often in a group setting, the siblings can bring off their interaction quite cordially. If they were forced to live together again, it could well be that the old tensions and conflict would become manifest once more.

The feelings of people towards their spouse's siblings can also effect the sibling relationship. This is yet another example of the importance of viewing kinship as a network of social relationships. We saw in the case of Mrs Barnes and her brother Terry how the spouse–sibling relationship can draw the siblings closer. The process can also work the other way. Townsend remarks: 'There were sometimes special reasons for the weaker relationship. Some women did not visit their brothers much because they did not like their wives' (1963, p. 120). Firth and his associates saw the 'third party element of spouses' as the second of the major reasons for severe breaking of sibling relationships. 'There were instances where relations with the sibling were definitely worsened or severed because of difficulties with the sibling's husband or wife' (1970, p. 432). They give numerous examples of this (pp. 428, 432) which are broadly similar to accounts gathered in the Selden Hey research. While feelings such as these affect the character and situation of interaction, it is important to realise again that interaction of some sort usually does occur for the reasons just given above: (1) the effect of other members of the network; and (2) the limited requirements of sibling interaction.

So far I have discussed the effects of negative affect, of disliking and a lack of compatibility between siblings or the spouses of siblings. I want now to turn to those sibling relationships which differ from the norm because of positive affect and a high degree of compatibility between those concerned. In a passage quoted earlier Adams implied that friendship between siblings in adulthood occurs most frequently in the working class (1970, p. 583). What little evidence there is available from previous research supports this contention. Young and Willmott, for example, suggest that in large families 'there seems to be a special tie with the "nearest sibling"'. They quote a respondent as saying: 'When we go out, there's always the six of us, my husband and me, my sister and her husband, and my brother and his girlfriend – and the children of course. If we have a party it's always the same six' (1962, p. 80). On the other hand Firth et al., despite an extended discussion of sibling relationships, make no mention of their middle-class respondents regarding their siblings as friends. They describe a small number of sibling relationships which appear to be emotionally close but give no indication whether these involve a high degree of sociability or whether other aspects of kin ideology are more important. For example, they indicate the strength of one relationship by describing how the siblings had agreed that they would look after the other's children if, by chance, the latter were orphaned (1970, p. 431). Certainly they nowhere imply that a high degree of sociability is a characteristic feature of many of these sibling relationships.

The Selden Hey research also supported Adams's view, though rather more dramatically than the above. There was a marked tendency for the working-class respondents to have a very significant relationship with one (and in two cases more than one) particular sibling. The implicit rules of relevance of these relationships were not limited to occasional visits and knowledge of each other's general welfare, as most sibling relationships were, but were defined much more widely. A greater range of social activities were included and the emphasis was placed on the enjoyment gained through interaction rather than on maintaining contact for its own sake. Without exception these siblings were recognised by the respondent as being the most important people in their sociable networks, and were frequently described as their 'best friends', despite the general inappropriateness of this label for kin relationships. In all, seven of the nineteen working-class respondents with siblings had a particularly strong and significant relationship with one of their siblings, and two respondents, Mr and Mrs Caswell, appeared to have relationships of this sort with more than one sibling. In addition, according to his wife's account, one of the husbands who declined to be interviewed had a similar relationship with one of his siblings. The most noticeable structural feature about all these relationships was that they occurred between siblings of the same sex, and (apart from the Caswells, of course) always with the one nearest in birth order to the respondents.

The example given at the beginning of this section of Mr Knowles's relationship with his brother Peter is representative of these special sibling relationships. It is clearly very different from the type of sibling relationship outlined above in the types of activity and range of setting seen as relevant to it. These spcial sibling relationships tend to reflect the gender differences apparent in non-kin relationships. Interaction between brothers more frequently took place in settings explicitly defined as sociable and enjoyable (e.g. a dance, a social club, a meal in a restaurant) while that between sisters tended to occur more within their homes. It was probably significant that in eight of the working-class cases that fit the category 'special' sibling relationship the sibling lived within 10 miles of Selden Hey. Interaction was consequently easy to organise. However, it would appear that geographical separation does not necessarily destroy these sibling relationships. Even where the siblings live some distance apart they can still regard each other as their closest friend and manipulate circumstances to encourage as frequent an interaction as possible. Thus one respondent claimed his brother, who lived in Derby, as his closest friend. More impressively, as well as spending all their holidays with Mr

Barrett's brother and his wife, Mr and Mrs Barrett travelled to Kent, where his brother lived, or else entertained them in Selden Hey, as frequently as they could for weekend visits.

An important aspect of nearly all the working-class respondents' 'special' sibling relationships was the spouse's relationship to the sibling and to the sibling's spouse. As with negative feelings, the network effect is operative. Thus in the case just cited Mrs Barrett said of her husband's brother and his wife: 'They're our real friends. They're the ones we do everything with.' The use of the plural throughout is indicative of her role in cementing her husband's relationship with his sibling. This factor was important in all the cases in which both the siblings in the 'special' relationship were married.

While five of the middle-class respondents had a relationship with a sibling that was characterised by a higher degree of compatibility and positive affection than was usual, none of these five was anything like as involved with his or her siblings as the above working-class respondents were. These relationships were different from the remaining sibling relationships in that they were recognised as being similar to friend relationships, but they were far less central to the organisation of these respondents' sociable lives than the working-class respondents' 'special' sibling relationships were to theirs.

Only in two of the five middle-class cases did the siblings live within 10 miles of one another. Consequently extensive interaction was less likely for these sibling relationships. Nevertheless the impression given was that even if they had lived closer these siblings would not have been as involved in the respondents' lives as were the 'special' siblings of the working-class respondents.

Structurally these middle-class relationships differed from the working-class ones in a number of interesting ways. First, and least important, in two cases the sibling relationship was between twins. None of the working-class siblings had been twins. Secondly, in two of the five cases the major bond was not between siblings but between respondents and their siblings-in-law. It is doubtful if either of these sibling relationships would have developed the way they had if the respondents had not found the sibling-in-law to be so compatible and come to regard him or her as a friend. (Note in both these cases the siblings were not of the same gender, so that the close siblings-in-law were.) In the third case, a respondent said enthusiastically when I asked him if he considered his wife's sister's husband a friend: 'Oh yes, definitely. Thoroughly, yes.' His wife added: 'If it wasn't for these two getting on so well, I don't suppose I'd see anywhere near as much of (my sister) as I do.' These examples illustrate yet again how kin relationships can only be understood when viewed as part of a network of relationships.

The Selden Hey sample was too small to warrant generalising from these results. None the less, it is of interest that these differences occurred and that they appear to support what little evidence there is on this matter in previous research.

SECONDARY KIN

Secondary kin, i.e. those kin not in a person's elementary families of origin or procreation, are of comparatively little importance in people's patterns of sociability, so need not detain us long. Interestingly, the principles that lie behind their organisation are similar in some respects to those that structure sibling relationships. The position here is affected, however, by the variation there is in the number of secondary kin known and met. Numerous studies have analysed this variation. In Britain the work of Firth and his associates has been particularly important. In their study of middle-class kinship the number of kin their respondents recognised ranged from 7 to 388 (Firth et al., 1970, p. 159). Similarly, in his earlier work with Djamour, Firth reports that the number of kin known to a household varied from 37 to 246 (1956, p. 38). Williams too reports that the number of kin recognised by his Ashworthy informants ranged from none to 202 (1963, p. 164). Even in the Selden Hey research, where little emphasis was placed on collating information about socially moribund kin relationships, the number of kin reported varied from 32 to 136.

As the number of kin recognised depends on biological as well as social factors, the range of kin known and seen is a more interesting factor, especially when kinship in Britain is contrasted with other kinship systems. Certainly compared with non-industrialised societies the range of kin interacted with is extremely small. As Firth found, it does not generally go beyond first cousins and their elementary families. Genealogically more distant kin play virtually no part at all in people's lives, being seen rarely even when known about, except perhaps at funerals or when they live in the same locality. As the concern in this text is with active sociability, those kin will not be considered further. (The grandparent–grandchild relationship will also be ignored here as there is a paucity of data concerning adult grandchildren.)

Within the categories of kin known and met, the actual relationships sustained vary quite widely. The key point here is that relationships with secondary kin are in Firth's words *permissive* rather than *obligatory* (1956, p. 14). There are no fixed 'rules' that govern the behaviour of these kin towards one another, no set of standard obligations demanded of them. Consequently personal selectivity and choice are basic to these relationships, as they are with sibling relationships. However, in the great majority of cases this selectivity and choice is tempered both by the fact that kinship acts as a social network and by features of social organisation I have chosen to label 'structured chance'.

As far as aunts, uncles, nephews, nieces and cousins are concerned, perhaps the primary point to make is that they play a very minor part in people's patterns of sociability. In the main these kin are met comparatively rarely, and when interaction does occur it is often perceived as a consequence of fortuitous circumstance rather than conscious design. Whereas friendship is concerned with enjoyment, and sibling solidarity with maintaining contact, the rules of relevance applied to the majority of secondary kin relationships stress little apart from being friendly when fortune brings you together. And it is perhaps worth noting that fortune does not always act thus. Unlike sibling relationships where a total lack of contact is rare, a proportion of known aunts, uncles, nephews, nieces and cousins are never seen. For example, in the north London study, there was no contact between Firth *et al.*'s respondents and approximately 40 per cent of their parents' siblings (1970, p. 201). The equivalent figure for the Selden Hey respondents was 27 per cent. In addition, the Selden Hey respondents had no contact at all with 60 per cent of their adult first cousins.

Some of these kin do not interact with each other because of personal or family friction and disagreement. However, the majority do not interact because circumstance never brings them together. They live their lives without crossing each other's paths. Conversely, where there is interaction between secondary kin, it is very frequently a consequence of those kin happening to be brought together by particular circumstances which they perceive to be partially incidental to their meeting. That is, in a majority of cases interaction results from these kin coming across each other whilst engaging in activities which are undertaken for reasons other than that of intentionally servicing this particular kin relationship. In such cases the kin bond is activated but not solely for its own sake. This feature of secondary kin organisation is brought out particularly well by Young and Willmott (1962) and is also apparent in Firth *et al.*'s report (1970). Like the Selden Hey respondents, theirs appear frequently to have implied that interaction with secondary kin was often to some degree a haphazard and chance affair. The main point to note here, however, is that while interaction frequently does depend on chance events, these events are not random. In other words, it is not a pure chance that is at work here, but rather a *structured chance*. By structured chance I mean that while interaction is unplanned and not purposeful as far as the interactants are concerned, it is nevertheless consequent upon principles of organisation which are integral to their social, and especially kinship, behaviour.

Basically there appear to be three major principles that are important here. First, a number of ceremonies in our culture traditionally embody a high degree of kin involvement. Weddings, funerals, christenings to a lesser extent, silver and gold wedding anniversaries are examples. If one is invited to these events because of a kin connection to the principal actors, it is not surprising that others of one's kin will be invited for the same reasons, and will consequently be seen there. Secondly, because, as mentioned above, secondary kin have intermediary primary and secondary kin in common with one another, occasionally both are likely to be interacting with the intermediary kin simultaneously and thus with each other. This is especially the case, it would appear, at Christmas, which is traditionally a time when kin come together and visit one another. The third principle which structures 'chance' meetings and makes them more likely appears to apply particularly to working-class respondents, especially those who have been geographically immobile. Such people tend to have a number of secondary kin living close to them. These kin are occasionally seen in passing. Interaction is not planned but it takes place because these kin happen quite often to be in the same place at the same time. As with the other two factors this third one makes 'chance' meetings more likely to occur. Thus the concept 'structured chance' accounts for the many secondary kin relationships in which interaction is not planned but which nevertheless takes place from time to time.

While the majority of interaction between secondary kin can be characterised as consequent on structured chance, not all the relationships subsumed here are equivalent. Relationships dependent totally on family ceremony, normally involving little more than the ritual questions and answers about family, health, and weather that occur when people who know one another only slightly have to interact because of external circumstances, are qualitatively different from those in which interaction results from purposeful visits to a sibling/parent third party. None the less, these latter relationships are still of limited significance in people's sociable lives except where the sibling–parent bond is a particularly strong one. Indeed, while data in comparable form are not presented in previous studies, less than an eighth of the Selden Hey respondents' uncles, aunts, nephews and nieces and a tenth of the cousins were of any importance in their patterns of sociability. In addition only slightly more than half the respondents were involved in such relationships. While personal liking was the key to some of these more significant relationships, the most important feature was the relationship of the intermediary siblings involved. Again in this respect the network effect of kinship is operative. Two examples will illustrate this. The first concerns Mrs Richardson's mother's brothers, Don and Henry, who both lived with their mother (Mrs Richardson's grandmother). As Mrs Richardson's mother and grandmother were sociably highly involved with one another, and as Mrs Richardson was very fond of her grandmother, she was seen whenever Mrs Richardson stayed with her mother in Stafford. As a consequence of this interaction Don and Henry were seen a good deal as they were often also present in their mother's home. A second example is provided by Mrs Knowles's father's brother and sister, Dick and Grace. Like Mrs Knowles's parents, both Dick and Grace, and their spouses, live in Selden Hey, all three couples having houses near to one another at the opposite end of the village to Mr and Mrs Knowles's house. Whenever Mrs Knowles visits her parents – four or five times a week – she is likely also to meet some or all of her aunts and uncles. She does not go over specifically to see them, but often does as a consequence of their being involved sociably with her parents. In these examples – which are typical of three-quarters of the more important aunt, uncle, nephew and niece relationships – it is evident that interaction occurs mainly, though not solely, with and through others, principally genealogically intermediary kin. It is usually only because the relationship of the aunt/uncle with her/his sibling is close that the relationship of aunt/uncle with nephew/niece takes on the characteristics it does.

In some cases, especially those involving single or childless and widowed aunts, a degree of responsibility may be felt for these kin, the more so as they become elderly. Where they have been known well all one's life, a moral obligation persists to maintain the relationship with them and allow them to continue to know a good deal about one's life situation. It is worth noting here that such a responsibility to an aunt can be felt without her necessarily being liked as a person. Indeed, more generally, being fond of particular secondary kin is not as central for determining the nature of the relationship one has with them as it is, for example, for the relationship one has with neighbours. This again is because of the importance of intermediary relationships for determining the nature of secondary kin relationships. When the pattern of interaction is defined by the relationships between others, then personal liking is likely to play a smaller part than otherwise.

Conversely, secondary kin can be liked a good deal without a particularly active relationship ensuing. In the Selden Hey research there were only five (out of a total of 299) aunt/uncle–nephew/niece relationships that involved a high degree of both personal liking and sociability. In these five cases, the respondents liked their relatives as the people they were and enjoyed being with them. Consequently interaction occurred purposefully and quite frequently simply because it was enjoyed. The activities involved were not limited to those normally associated with kinship; the people were known because they were kin but were seen because they were liked. For example, Mr Cullen and his wife's nephew, James, both worked in London, so quite frequently met for lunch sometimes with and sometimes without their wives. James and his wife spent weekends at the Cullens' house in Selden Hey five or six times a year, and occasionally they all went to the theatre together in London. It is this kind of sociable involvement, removed from any over-riding kinship connotations, that typified the nature of these five relationships. It must be stressed in conclusion that such cases comprise a very small minority of aunt/uncle–nephew/niece relationships.

Because of the greater likelihood of age similarity it might be supposed that, of all secondary kin, cousins are the most likely to become thought of as friends. In fact there is little evidence in the research literature to suggest this is at all typical. Certainly, as Firth *et al.* point out, most people show 'discrimination between individual cousins on the basis of propinquity, compatibility of temperament and interests, response to the wishes of parents, aunts or uncles' (1970, pp. 444–5), but few cousins are important figures in each other's sociable networks. In the Selden Hey research only six out of the 392 adult first cousins known to the respondents were regarded as friends in their own right. In three of these cases the cousins were counted as amongst the respondents' closest friends. As with the aunt, uncle, nephew and niece relationships discussed in the previous paragraph, the fact these people were members of a kin network was incidental to their friendship. A further six of the respondents' cousins could be characterised as important figures in their sociability networks though they were not regarded as friends. In these the relationship was based more directly on the fact of kinship. One illustration of such a relationship was Janet Parry's with her cousin Larry. Larry's mother and Janet's mother were close to one another, and so Janet and Larry had always known one another quite well, as is suggested by Janet's being godmother to one of Larry's two children. However, neither Janet nor her husband found Larry or his wife particularly interesting. As she said: 'They're not the sort of people you'd go out for a drink with. We visit them when we stay with my parents, but really it's only because my mother makes us. She says things like "Don't you think you should go and see Larry?", so usually we do sometime or other in our stay.' While sociably more significant than the great majority of secondary kin, it is clear that such relationships are not equivalent to friendships. They are not freely chosen but are largely consequent on the strength of intermediate kin relationships.

Chapter 8

The Structure of Sociability

'One of the main obstacles to [a dynamic theory of social bonding]
is the relative looseness, not to say vagueness, of many of the
technical terms currently used in the sociological and anthropological literature if one refers to the way people are linked to
each other in societies. Many of these terms suffer from a characteristic sociological disease: they are shrouded in a voluntaristic
twilight. They blur the distinction between human bonds that can
be made and unmade at will by those concerned, and human bonds
which cannot be made and unmade at will. Durkheim's use of the
term "organic solidarity" is a good example of this twilight . . .
More recent examples are concepts like "role", "interaction" and
the ubiquitous "human relations". Their use can easily give the
impression that the central task of sociology is to study how
individual people act or behave when they make contact or form
relations with each other. The implications appear to be that human
beings are always free to act, to interact, to form relationships as
they like. In actual fact their ability to do this is limited and
sociological studies are very much concerned with the problem of
how limited it is and why.' (Elias, 1973, pp. xvii–xviii).

Out of the twilight?
Norbert Elias's intention in the paper from which this extract is
taken is to emphasise that many social relations can neither be
created nor broken at will. They are given by the societal structures
that exist independently of any of the individuals party to them.
Thus, for example, the essential features of the slave–slave-owner
relationship, the serf–feudal-lord relationship and the employee-
employer relationship are written into the socio-economic systems
under which they operate and consequently none of the individuals
involved in them is free to restructure them as he pleases. The
forms of such relationships are embedded in a moral, legal and
economic code which acts as a social fact, in the Durkheimian sense,
external to the individual yet constraining his behaviour. Many
other types of social relations, both between individuals and, perhaps

more important, between groups of individuals, are similarly constrained. Many involve, to use Elias's term, 'interdependencies' which bind the two sides together in a way neither has willed or planned. Of course, the extent to which this happens, the extent to which individuals are constrained in their social relations, varies. It is consequently important to 'distinguish between interdependencies which people can bring about, up to a point, voluntarily and deliberately . . . and interdependencies by which they are bound but which they cannot individually enter or break at will' (Elias, 1973, p. xviii).

The relationships this book is concerned with, kin and non-kin sociable relations, are clearly closer to the first of these two polar types. They are those over which the individual, as of right, exercises some degree of choice. The very approach adopted here, with its emphasis on the way sociable relationships are actively constructed and created by those involved, highlights this. None the less, Elias's concerns are still relevant, for although each person appears free to shape particular sociable relationships according to his own desires, these relationships are, individually and collectively, still structured by a variety of factors external to them. The influence of some of these factors, for example, class membership, family-cycle position and the presence of closed kinship networks, has been examined to differing degrees in the preceding chapters. The strands of argument developed in them will be consolidated and extended in this one.[1] The importance of the chapter, in line with Elias's comments, is that it complements the voluntaristic stance of earlier chapters by focusing on the structural determinants of sociable networks as on-going systems of relationships.

EXTERNAL ASPECTS OF SOCIABILITY NETWORKS

We can begin by noting that there is quite wide variation in the sociable lives led by different people. Sociable patterns diverge markedly with respect both to the amount and type of sociable activity engaged in. Some people are highly active sociably, interacting with numerous others in numerous settings; other people are, through choice or circumstance, extremely isolated. In this, patterns of sociability reflect leisure proclivities more generally (Parker, 1976). However, given this variation we can also note that the sociable activities of most adults tend to be patterned in a repetitive manner. They tend to involve regular, repeated events with the same associates, and to be concentrated at the weekend. A range of people may be met and various types of activity enjoyed on occasions, but overall it is the few recurrent situations undertaken with the same people which predominate. To put this another way, most people's 'funds of sociability' are limited. By far the greater part of their time not spent working or sleeping is spent 'doing nothing' or, more accurately, doing those normal, unremarkable things that do not involve people outside the household unit but which are enjoyed in, or required by, the organisation of routine domestic life.

The variation evident in the range of different people's sociable activities is structured by the same factors as affect their wider life-styles. From Durkheim and Tönnies onwards, these factors have been of interest to sociologists, particularly those specialising in urban and community sociology. In this respect the most influential approach has probably been that of the 'human ecologists'. Under the auspices of Park and Burgess at the University of Chicago in the 1920s and 1930s – a time and place characterised by large-scale urban expansion – location within a spatial structure came to be taken as the key to explaining forms of life-style. This idea has been heavily criticised in recent years. As well as the more radical critics who argue that industrial capitalism rather than urbanisation is the key process in generating forms of social relation in Western society (see Pickvance, 1976), a number of writers have suggested that location is only significant to the extent that the mechanisms of the housing and land markets congregate people with similar life-chances and interests in the same area. They argue that many of the traits associated by the human ecologists with location can be explained more directly by considering the social characteristics of those involved. Along with many others, both Gans (1968) and Pahl (1968), for example, emphasis *social class, geographical mobility,* and *family-cycle position* as amongst the key features in determining ways of life. We can add a fourth variable, that of *gender,* to this list.

SOCIAL CLASS

As has been noted throughout this book, the effects of social class on sociability are most pervasive. While the basic equation of non-manual and manual work with middle-class and working-class membership is extremely crude, it none the less serves to distinguish the discrete ways in which the middle class and working class organise their various sociable relationships. Like many of the other differences between these two sectors of the population, this variation relates to their different material and occupational circumstances. The financial and temporal constraints imposed by these factors shape their patterns of sociability as much as they do all other aspects of their way of life. This has been widely recognised with regard to primary kin relationships. The flow of material goods between middle-class and working-class parents and their adult children tends to be quite different due to the different resources available to the parents and the distinct career-cycles involved. As Bell has demonstrated, the middle-class father is generally able to assist his children quite substantially in creating a middle-class lifestyle by providing material gifts, especially for grandchildren, that help stretch the young couple's own limited resources farther.

In addition, though, the tendency for working-class and middle-class members respectively to define their non-kin sociable relationships as dependent or independent of particular contexts and settings would seem to be consequent, in part at least, upon the resources they have available for sociability. Essentially containing relationships within specific contexts allows the working class a greater control over their relationships through limiting the demands others can legitimately make. It curbs the exchange basis of the relationships. Similarly not using the home for non-kin sociability means that quite large areas of one's life are defined as irrelevant to these relationships and consequently also allows a greater control to be exercised over them. In turn, the discrete ways of defining relationships can be maintained because of the class homophily of non-kin sociability.

Middle- and working-class sociable networks also differ in their geographical spread. Working-class kin and non-kin networks both tend to be more localised than middle-class ones. In part, middle-class non-kin networks are less localised because of their members' greater geographical mobility. However, this is not the only reason. As Pahl (1968) has outlined, the middle class, because of their material advantages, can overcome the constraints of place with less difficulty than the working class. In particular, their higher rate of car ownership (see Halsey, 1972) means that they can keep non-local relationships extant more easily. In addition, the tendency for the working class to organise relationships around particular contexts reinforces this process as the sociable relationships they develop in one setting are generally not maintained once that setting is left. As the majority of contexts in which working-class sociability occurs are local, the consequence is that non-kin networks themselves tend to be localised.

Over and above these basic class divisions, particular occupations impose their own constraints on patterns of sociability, as has been mentioned in earlier chapters. Factors like the hours and regularity of work, the arduousness of it, the time spent travelling to work, the control the worker has over the when and where of its performance, the unspecified, semi- or unofficial, extra-curricula sociable activities required by some occupations, and so on, are all likely to shape and constrain each worker's pattern of sociability to some degree. Such factors are also likely to constrain the worker's spouse, certainly in as far as joint sociable activities are concerned.

The individual's occupation can affect sociable patterns more positively. Not only is work a major source of sociable companions, but the workplace itself provides a continuing setting for some forms of sociable interaction. Bearing in mind the tendency of the working class to limit their sociable interaction with particular others to given social situations, this latter function is all the more important. The opportunities open for sociable contact at work differ, of course, according to the nature of the work and the control one has over it. At the risk of overgeneralising, we can note that in this respect most non-manual workers are in a better position than most manual employees, while that of full-time housewives and mothers is ambiguous in that they control their work setting but are socially isolated in it. Equally, the particular way work relationships are developed depends on the factors discussed above as well as on the individual's overall orientation to the workplace (see Goldthorpe *et al.*, 1969). But even though some workers undoubtedly have primarily an instrumental attitude to their work, for most people it none the less provides an opportunity to initiate sociable interaction in whatever form they take to be normal.

FAMILY- AND LIFE-CYCLE POSITION

The stage reached in the family- and life-cycle can also affect the individual's pattern of sociability. As discussed in Chapter 5, the child-rearing and retirement stages appear to be the two that constrain sociability most. The arguments presented there do not need to be rehearsed in this chapter. Rather we can focus more on the way these stages in the family- and life-cycle affect kin and non-kin relationships respectively.

Young children influence their parents' sociability habits in a number of ways. Apart from anything else, their very presence makes some forms of sociability more difficult. Indeed, in our society children are to a degree segregated from much adult sociability, especially non-kin sociability. Sociability with non-kin, with its emphasis on enjoyment, often occurs in settings such as pubs or clubs of one form or another from which children are explicitly excluded. Most sociability with non-kin also occurs in the evening, a time when children are unlikely to be present. The consequences of this exclusion of children are obvious enough. Either the parents are sociable independently of each other; or babysitters are arranged; or sociability occurs in the home. We saw in previous chapters how this last option is typical of middle-class patterns but not of working-class ones. Working-class couples are more likely to solve this problem by establishing independent sociable habits, as suggested by some of the illustrative material in Chapter 6, or alternatively by using kin, especially mothers if they live locally, as regular babysitters. Middle-class couples, partly because they are more mobile, tend to use non-kin more frequently as babysitters either on a paid basis or through informal exchange with other parents.

While children constrain sociability in these ways, we should not lose sight of the fact established in previous chapters that children can facilitate sociable interaction by bringing their parents into contact with others in a similar situation. As we have seen, this may be particularly important for full-time housewives and mothers who would otherwise be sociably isolated. However, children are perhaps even more influential in cementing kin relationships. In contrast to non-kin, sociability with kin normally includes children. The emphasis in kin relationships is on maintaining contact rather than on enjoyment *per se*. Far from being excluded, children as members of the kin group become a focus of interaction and a mechanism for increasing the solidarity of the kin group. Frequently their presence encourages rather than limits interaction, especially between their parents and their grandparents. As we have seen, it is partly through gifts to grandchildren that middle-class parents help maintain their children's living standards, and it is not by chance that working-class mother–adult-daughter relationships become most active at this stage in the daughter's family-cycle.

In the retirement stage of the life-cycle, the processes are rather different. To begin with, sociability, whatever form it takes, becomes more exacting. The effort involved is that bit harder as old age and possible infirmity have their effect. Yet at the same time sociability in itself becomes even more important than at previous stages in the life-cycle. To the extent that there is disengagement from the various settings that previously gave them their sense of social identity, the elderly are forced to rely more heavily on sociability in a pure form as a means of ensuring their status in society. Not only are they likely to have more 'free time' on their hands, but their integration into society's wider social structures will depend less on their positions in formal institutions and more on their informal bonds of sociability. Whereas previously these latter would have been more peripheral to their social being, it will now increasingly be mediated through them.

For this reason both kin and non-kin relationships should in theory receive renewed emphasis in old age. The issue is not simple, however. Precisely because one is less embedded in societal institutions than previously the creation, and indeed the servicing, of non-kin sociability becomes more difficult, for as we have seen such institutions play a major part in the formation and continuation of many of these relationships. Disengagement effectively means that the pool of others one is sociable with cannot be enlarged. More important perhaps, it means that when people leave that pool because of death or because they are no longer party to the setting in which they were seen, they cannot readily be replaced by others. Thus the elderly person's non-kin sociable network inevitably shrinks, despite tending to be of increased personal and social significance.

It is for similar reasons that Cumming and Schneider (1961) suggest that sibling relationships become more significant in old age. This may well be so in many cases but is likely to depend on factors such as geographical proximity, the number of siblings available and the character of the sibling relationship in previous stages of the life-cycle. However, in general it would seem that the elderly emphasise *inter*generational kin sociability rather more than such *intra*generational sociability. The figures who are most important in providing meaning in old age are children and grandchildren. As numerous studies have demonstrated, it is the elderly without descendent kin who are the most isolated and the most lonely. Griffith Hughes of Rosser and Harris's 'Hughes Family Morriston' captured this nicely when he said of his grandchildren: 'Well there of course is the real tie. You like to have your grandchildren about you and see them grow up and get on' (Rosser and Harris, 1965, p. 14). In this statement Mr Hughes is implicitly recognising the structural importance of descendent kin bonds for keeping the elderly involved, at least peripherally, in mainstream societal structures and processes. The extent to which these kin bonds can substitute for and replace previous associations depends of course on a variety of factors including the geographical distribution of the kin and the stages they have reached in their own family- and life-cycle. However, generally it is the case that descendent kin play a large part in patterns of sociability in the final phase of the life-cycle. This is so notwithstanding the fact that the dependencies involved in the relationships are asymmetrical with the elderly needing these kin rather more than the latter need them.

GEOGRAPHICAL MOBILITY

Many of the consequences of geographical mobility have been discussed at some length in previous chapters and consequently need not be developed here. As is well known, the middle class tend to be more geographically mobile than the working class in terms of both distance and frequency of move. The career pattern labelled by Watson (1964) as 'spiralist' highlights the contingencies of occupational structure largely responsible for this. As noted earlier, one consequence of this is that middle-class sociable networks are rather more dispersed geographically than working-class ones. There are important differences between kin and non-kin networks in this respect. As developed in Chapter 5, only a minority of middle-class friendships survive actively for long after one side moves any distance away, even though the typical organisation of middle-class friendships encourages such survival more than the normal form of working-class sociable relationship does. Resources for sociability are limited, so gradually but inevitably the relationships developed in the old locality get replaced by relationships created in the new one. In the end only 'true friendships', tautologically defined, can overcome the disruptive effect of distance.

Primary kin relationships, on the other hand, persist despite geographical separation. Where parents and/or siblings do not live near at hand, they are normally visited or entertained for weekend or longer holiday periods. As described in Chapter 7, parents often act as centres of an interaction and communication network when some or all of their children have been mobile. When parents and siblings live locally there is of course no need for extended visits and consequently patterns of interaction are significantly different.

One further point that warrants mention is that 'collective' geographical mobility affects patterns of sociability somewhat differently from 'individual' mobility. When a number of people move into adjacent new homes simultaneously there tends to be a 'rush' on sociability, as numerous research projects have reported (see Thorns, 1972, for a summary). Neighbours appear keen to know one another and assist each other in the numerous difficulties faced in 'wearing in' a new house and cultivating as gardens ground which has until recently been a muddy building site. As social life becomes more established and sociable networks more extensive, relationships settle down through a gradual process of selection and rejection. The urgency of the original sociability dissipates and only the more satisfying relationships continue to be serviced. People who move into a house in an already established area are faced by this rather different situation in which other people's sociable networks are already complete. They are usually the only ones moving and the only ones who need to create new relationships. The battles with nature and the builders have already been fought, so the communal consciousness and consequent *bonhomie* of a quasi-frontier setting is missing.

GENDER DIFFERENCES

We saw in Chapter 5 that there is some debate in the literature over whether middle-class friendship formation is dominated by husbands or wives. In contrast there can be no doubt that a range of leisure pursuits involving sociability are, in our society, more readily available to males than to females. The 'opportunity structures' of leisure open to females are far more constrained. As Parker notes, the differences here 'reflect the differences in role which have historically been ascribed to men and women'. He continues: 'The traditional, home-based existence of women, their lower educational status, their primary role as home-maker and mother, their second-class legal status, the comparatively sheltered condition of adolescent women and the differences in standards regarding sexual activity have all played a part in accounting for the difference in the leisure of women and men' (1976, p. 87). There are two related issues warranting discussion here: the facilities available for sociability, and the consequences of the conventional domestic division of labour.

Even the more optimistic analysts of changes in gender-based inequalities are forced to recognise that many settings for sociability are male preserves. Rather than being merely a 'hiccup' in the inevitable development of equality, many sociologists see this phenomenon as a quite central element of continuing male domination. In this light, the relative paucity of female sports, the male bias of pubs and social clubs, the right of males of all ages to go out alone or in groups all reflect the wider societal constraints under which females are forced to operate. In contrast to female patterns, male sociability is more wide-ranging and independent. This can be seen by considering sociability in social clubs and public houses. In general women are not positively excluded from such settings but within them they tend to be less than equal. Often the normative pressures internalised over a life-time's socialisation result in females feeling inhibited from even entering them unless accompanied by a male and out of place if they do so. Whitehead's study of a Here-fordshire pub brilliantly illustrates the processes lying behind this (1976). While the mechanisms of male social control she describes, which included teasing, jeering, propositioning and sexual horse-play, may be extreme, they none the less still occur in modified form more widely. Collectively the results of such pressure reinforcing cultural ideas of appropriate male and female behaviour are that females feel, indeed are made to feel, socially dependent on males, and that their opportunities for non-domestic sociability are curtailed.

This male domination of external social activities is clearly related directly to the normal organisation of household tasks in the domestic division of labour. For better or for worse, housework and child care are generally taken in our society to be female responsibilities. Numerous studies have shown that when a wife is employed gainfully outside the home such duties remain unequally shared between her and her husband. If, as some would claim, husbands now participate more extensively in a range of household tasks than previously, the emphasis is still on 'helping the wife out' or 'lending her a hand' rather than on taking an equal share in the day-to-day running of the home. This is the more so when the wife is not employed but works as a housewife and mother full-time.

The point here is not simply that full-time housewives on average spend almost twice the time on housework that their husbands spend at work (see Oakley, 1974), but that the nature of their work, especially child-minding, results in their not having clearly defined hours. Unlike their husbands, whose work and leisure-time activities can be clearly differentiated from each other, the housewife with children tends to be 'on duty' more or less continuously. This continuous involvement in child-care and housework, with tasks never being completed once and for all, acts in concert with other concomitants of the female role, including wives' economic dependence on husbands and the generalised fear of being out alone, and ensures that the range of sociable activities open to women is more limited than those available to men. Despite any changes that may be occurring in our society, the woman's place far more than the man's is, in this sense, still in the home. Outside work hours, husbands have more freedom than their wives to come and go as they please and to associate with whom they wish.

The combination of limited provision for female sociability outside the home and the normative constraints binding them to the home results in males and females having different leisure habits and to some extent different patterns of sociability. Of course such differences will not occur in all marriages to the same extent. They will be least evident in couples who normally share leisure activities and sociable companions, and most marked amongst couples whose sociable lives are largely independent of each other. The effect of these factors will also depend on the extent to which the home is used as a centre for sociability. To some extent, middle-class females can compensate for the relative lack of provision for non-domestic sociability by entertaining non-kin in their homes. As we have seen, this is not a typical working-class form of sociability, so the opportunities for working-class wives to be sociable with non-kin independently of their husbands will tend to be more limited. Indeed, where working-class couples do lead independent sociable lives, we would expect the wife's sociable network to be dominated more by kin because of these constraints against sociability with non-kin. Kin are likely to be less central to the husband's network because he is freer to interact with non-kin in non-domestic settings. This indeed is the picture portrayed in studies of traditional working-class areas, where, in Bott's terms (1971), conjugal relationships tend to be segregated rather than joint.

INTERNAL ASPECTS OF SOCIABILITY NETWORKS

The four factors discussed here – class, family- and life-cycle position, geographical mobility and gender – are amongst the most basic that structure social life in general and patterns of sociability in particular. As noted, urban sociologists especially have concentrated on them because of their greater power than ecological variables to explain differences in the ways of life people lead in cities and suburbs. They are, of course, all 'external', independent variables in that they affect patterns of sociability but are not affected directly by them. They are, as it were, 'givens' which shape sociability by limiting the choices and options available to people. However, not all the factors that are held to structure sociability are of this form. We also need to consider the effects of factors *internal* to sociability networks. The point here is that the organisation of particular elements in a network may itself affect the way in which other elements within it are developed. Thus, for example, in Chapter 7 it was shown that sibling relationships could only be understood as part of a larger network of primary kin relationships. Similarly, in any cohesive social group, any two people's relationship to each other is likely to be affected by their relationships to others in the group. The mechanisms of informal social control operating in small communities as diverse as Nuer settlements and Hutterite colonies work precisely because of this. Not only is each individual dependent upon the co-operation of the others in the group for his life's needs, but relationships tend to be multiplex. Consequently a disagreement or conflict in one relationship will have repercussions on others and potentially disrupt many areas of social life.

The most pertinent framework for examining the internal structuring of sociability is network analysis. The rest of this chapter will be concerned with the issues raised by it. The approach will necessarily be more critical, and in this sense more negative, than in the first half of this chapter as the ideas to be considered are at the same time more speculative and complex than those discussed earlier. While the aim is still to understand how patterns of sociability are structured, the focus will be more directly on evaluating the potential contribution of network analysis than on the specific effects of particular variables.

NETWORK ANALYSIS

In recent years a number of urban and family sociologists have recognised that the concept of 'social network' has great potential for explaining the organisation of sociability. If this potential remains strangely unfulfilled, it must be in part because collecting adequate and full data on social networks is so difficult and time-consuming, the more so when information is required not just on those an individual knows (his first order star, in Barnes's 1969 terminology), but also on which of these people know one another (his personal network or first order zone). However, such method-ological problems are only a part of the reason why network studies have so far failed to live up to their promise, particularly with respect to the sociology of friendship and kinship. Conceptual issues that have not as yet been adequately clarified by network analysts are of at least equal importance.

As Barnes (1972, p. 2) notes: 'The basic idea behind both the metaphorical and the analytical uses of social networks [is] that the configuration of cross-cutting interpersonal bonds is in some unspecified way causally connected with the actions of these per-sons and with the social institutions of their society.' In this respect network analysis is thus nothing more than an 'orienting state-ment' that can be used in combination with a number of theoretical frameworks for analysing a range of social behaviour. The particular issue we are concerned with here is the extent to which individual sociable relationships are structured and shaped by the total sets of sociable relationships of which they are a part. Essentially this involves two distinct questions: (1) what is the configuration of any individual's personal network or first order zone? and (2) what effect do different configurations have on individual relationships? Neither of these questions is as easy to answer as might appear at first glance. The first question in particular contains many con-ceptual difficulties that are rather complex to unravel but which need to be unravelled if network analysis is to develop satisfactorily. The major difficulty is that, like the majority of sociologists and anthropologists studying kinship (see Keesing, 1972), most network analysts have yet to develop satisfactory ways of analysing qualita-tive aspects of relationships. They have tended to ignore, or rather assume as unproblematic, what makes a link in a network a link. For example, Boissevain (1972, p. 108), in his description of two Maltese informants' first order stars, includes people whom his informants know of but have never met. Such a practice certainly raises questions about what it is to 'know' someone, and what the features of a relationsip that are of importance in any given socio-logical enterprise are, questions which most network analysts, including Boissevain, have not attempted to answer (Mitchell, 1974). The difficulties raised by this can be clearly seen by consider-ing the work of Elizabeth Bott and the consequent research this generated. I am not so much interested in the validity of these studies here as with using them as a vehicle for discussing the com-plexity of the issues involved.

ELIZABETH BOTT

Elizabeth Bott's research concerned the relationship between con-jugal roles and the structure of social networks. On the basis of intensive fieldwork in London she classified conjugal relationships as either segregated or joint. She labelled them segregated when the husband and wife followed a rigid division of labour within the home, and joint when they shared domestic tasks and activities. (Segregated role relationships can themselves be subdivided into complementary, where the activities of husband and wife are distinct yet fit together to form a whole, and independent, where activities are carried out separately by husband and wife without reference to one another.) Likewise she categorised social networks on the basis of their 'connectedness' as being either 'loose-knit' or 'close-knit'. They are loose-knit when relatively few of the people included in them know and interact with one another, and close-knit when a high proportion of others in the network know and interact with each other. Elizabeth Bott hypothesised that: 'The degree of segregation in the role-relationship of husband and wife varies directly with the connectedness of the family's social network. The more connected the network, the greater the degree of segregation between the roles of husband and wife. The less connected the network, the smaller the degree of segregation between the roles of husband and wife' (1971, p. 60).

Bott explains this relationship between the connectedness or 'density' (see Barnes, 1969; Bott, 1971, p. 250) of networks and conjugal role relationships by positing: (1) that close-knit networks lead to a higher degree of normative consensus than loose-knit networks, so that individuals in them are consequently more constrained to conform to given standards of behaviour; and (2) that where spouses belong to close-knit networks they are less dependent on each other for emotional and other satisfactions because they can rely on the close-knit set of other relationships in which they are embedded. Where these relationships are more loose-knit, mutual assistance is likely to be 'more fragmented and less consistent' (Harris, 1969, p. 170; Kapferer, 1974, p. 86).

Without any doubt Bott's work has been most influential. As Harris notes, it has 'made impossible the proliferation of studies of the internal structure of the family which take no account of its social environment' (1969, p. 175). None the less, it has been criticised quite severely, every aspect of it seeming to have been questioned by one author or another at some time. For example, Platt (1969), Harrell-Bond (1969) and Toomey (1971) criticise the validity of a single measure of conjugality, suggesting that wide variation is found within any marriage between different spheres of domestic activity. Similarly Cubitt (1973) and Kapferer (1973) have questioned whether measuring the overall density of networks is a satisfactory operationalisation of networks' structural properties. The more important criticisms from the present perspective are those which challenge Bott's theoretical position.

One of the first papers to do this was Harold Fallding's 'The family and the idea of a cardinal role' (1961). After agreeing with Bott's premise that close-knit networks are likely to result in greater normative consensus, Fallding disputes her assertion that uniform external expectations invariably impose a standard of role segregation on spouses. He asks why the consensus should not encourage joint roles instead. Not finding any obvious answer to this question, Fallding reinterprets Bott's results. He suggests that if the apparently close-knit network of couples with segregated conjugal role-relationships is analysed separately for each of the spouses, then it would be found that both husband and wife were members of 'sex in-groups'. That is, 'a sharp cleavage by sex right across the network' would be discovered 'so that [the couple's combined networks could] hardly be called connected'. For Fallding, then, 'the role segregation of the sexes within the family goes with sexual segregation outside it' (1961, p. 342). Harris develops these points by demonstrating how Bott's explanation of the correlation between close-knit networks and segregated conjugal role-relationships depends on the sets of others with whom these husbands and wives individually interact constituting 'groups' in the sociological sense – that is to say [coming] to share valued ways of acting (norms) and a capacity for acting together'. 'Where this happens,' Harris continues, 'each spouse will have an interconnected network of relationships of the same kind, have outside sources of gratification through membership of a primary group, be able to mobilise resources through his group membership and be subjected to considerable pressure to conform to group norms' (1969, p. 172). Harris adds that where such groups are 'mono-sex groups', then, at least under some conditions, it is likely that marital roles will be segregated. In addition Fallding makes the point that the only reason the combined network of spouses with segregated conjugal role-relationships *appears* as close-knit overall rather than as being in two discrete segments – the husband's and the wife's – is because of kin relationships. In effect he argues that while people know and interact with their spouses' kin – and thus by Bott's criteria would include these people in their personal networks – this does not necessarily make these kin-in-law significant or influential others in their social lives.

In making these criticisms, Fallding and Harris are querying three of Bott's basic propositions: (1) that spouses' networks can always be analysed jointly in a meaningful way on the straightforward basis of whom each knows and sees; (2) that networks, in the sense of people known and seen, rather than groups, in the sense of a collection of people capable of acting in concert, are necessarily effective in exerting social control; and (3) that kin and non-kin can be treated as equivalent even though kinship 'naturally' as it were tends towards a closed network structure. These well-founded criticisms are rather more radical than they appear at first sight for they take issue with the fundamental assumption underlying Bott's stance: that the structure of social networks, irrespective of the exchange content of the individual relationships that make it up, affect people's behaviour. In essence, Fallding and Harris (amongst others) are pointing out that we cannot hypothesise about the effect on an individual's actions of the relationships to which he is party without paying some heed to the actual nature of these bonds. They are arguing that structure and content must be considered together. This can be taken a stage further because in fact structure and content are inevitably and inextricably linked together.

The idea of a social network is an analytical construct which involves making decisions about which individuals (or 'points' in the network) should be connected to one another. The grounds on which these decisions are made necessarily involve judgements about the content of the individual relationships in question: whether they are sufficiently active, whether they are sufficiently important, and so on. Ultimately, then, what Harris and Fallding are claiming is that Bott's (and, it must be added, other network analysts') common-sense criteria for including a link in a network, that of 'knowing and interacting with' another, are insufficient for the type of analysis she attempts. They are suggesting that by giving equal weight to different types of relationship within the network structures she maps out, Bott is led to focus on somewhat spurious correlations and consequently ignores the more important social processes that do really explain conjugal role relationships. If she had discriminated more between different types of relationship, she would have been able to portray more accurately the consequence of different network structures. But of course – and this is the central point in my argument – if she had so differentiated between different types of relationship, *ipso facto* the network structures she records would also have been changed. The configuration and shape of social networks, in other words, is not fixed and immutable, given once and for all to be reproduced by the analyst, but depends on what the analyst regards as constituting a 'link' for his or her purposes. Thus questions about the shape or structure of networks can only be answered with reference to the content of the relationships included in them. Basing networks, as Bott and most other network theorists do, on knowing and interacting with others is certainly not suitable for all problems that concern them. Further, indeed, it is a basis that by its very nature makes it likely that confused and incomplete analyses will result as the solution to a theoretical question appears in this light as a common-sense, self-evident matter.

From this, then, it is apparent that answering the first question posed above – 'what is the configuration of any individual's personal network?' – depends on analytical decisions made by the researcher. Similarly the answer to the second question – 'what effects do different configurations have on individual relationships?' – also quite obviously depends on these decisions. Equally important, the work of Fallding, Harris and others who have examined Bott's findings all show that the effect of such networks on behaviour depends on the nature of the relationships involved in it. This is the basic contention behind Harris's argument that Bott's theoretical account of the connection between close-knit networks and segregated conjugal role-relationships depends on members of the network forming groups capable of acting together. Perhaps the writer who makes this point most strongly is Kapferer, one of the more theoretically sophisticated of network analysts. Both in his early work on the relationships between men employed in a surface workshop of a Zambian mine and in his more recent work on social networks and conjugal relationships, Kapferer makes the content of relationships integral to his analysis. An examination of this latter study, which arises out of a concern with Bott's hypothesis, will illustrate the principles involved here (Kapferer, 1972).

By combining network analysis with exchange theory, Kapferer is able to argue convincingly that some networks Bott would classify as close-knit are more likely to lead to joint than independent conjugal role-relationships. Essentially Kapferer's argument is quite simple. He criticises Bott for treating the married couple's separate networks jointly and for concentrating on network density *per se* at the expense of other structural factors. For him the degree of star and zone cross-linkage between the husband's and wife's social networks are the key issues in determining conjugal role-relationships, especially when only those relationships to which the spouses are highly committed are considered. Where 'both husband and wife are directly linked by social relationships to the same individuals', and where 'the individuals located in the various zones of the respective networks are directly linked by social relationships to each other', then the role-relationship of spouses is likely to be joint or complementary rather than independent, the more so the more the individuals have 'invested' in these cross-linkages (Kapferer, 1973, p. 102).

Following Blau, Kapferer suggests each individual invests personal resources (energy, time, services, and so on) in his relationships for which he expects equivalent returns. Thus relationships are systems of exchange in which obligations are continually being created and discharged. Kapferer argues that where individuals participate in a common set of relationships, 'failure of one individual to discharge the obligations in his relationship to another will put the former's other relationships at risk . . . [for] the other individuals commonly connected to the two parties involved may expect an increased risk of failing to receive a return on their investment in their relationships with the individual concerned' (1972, p. 101). Given this, Kapferer's thesis is that where spouses' networks are characterised by a high degree of cross-linkage, 'each spouse is dependent on the other for the maintenance of trust in his social relationships and the continuance of these relationships' (1972, p. 103). Such joint responsibility for their set of social relationships and the spouses' consequent dependence on one another is, according to Kapferer, naturally compatible with a joint or complementary conjugal role-relationship. This is mainly because in comparison to the independent form these types of role-relationship allow each spouse greater control over the other so that the 'investments' each has made in their various other relationships are the more effectively safeguarded.

Like Harris's and Fallding's, Kapferer's argument is of interest here for what it suggests about network analysis in general rather than for the particular amendments it makes to Bott's hypothesis. We have already seen how the structure of social networks cannot be divorced from the content of the relationships making them up, and how consequently questions about the effect of network structure on individual relationships are barren unless the content of these relationships is considered at the same time. Kapferer's analysis is suggestive because it illustrates how different configurations of similar relationships are likely to influence the interactants' behaviour. Referring back to Elias's statement quoted at the beginning of this chapter, it enables us to examine the dependencies that exist in sets of equivalent relationships by focusing attention on those which can be less easily broken than others. Essentially Kapferer's argument is that relationships can be less easily altered when they are one of a close-knit set of similar relationships than when they are not part of such a set, especially if the relationships in question are multiplex and important to those involved. Failure to honour structurally isolated relationships is less likely to have consequences for one's other relationships than failure to honour structurally integrated relationships. The individual needs to be more careful of his 'investments' in these latter because potentially each can affect many others. Clearly the more important these integrated relationships are to the individual, the more he will be concerned with avoiding disruption to any one of them for fear such disruption will damage the balance of exchange in the others. Thus when an individual is embedded in a close-knit set of relationships of a particular type, he is indeed embedded. To the extent that they are important to him as a set, he is dependent upon and constrained by them in a way he would not be if there was no inter-linkage between them. Relatively, then, he is less free to alter their exchange basis, and less likely to develop new relationships, for any newcomer would need to prove acceptable to the network of others. Thus the more close-knit, the more group-like, any set of similar relationships to which an individual is party is, the more these relationships act as social facts, constraining and external, and consequently the less able is he to make or unmake them at will.

In fact we have already seen in Chapter 7 how this feature of close-knit networks operates with respect to primary kin and to a lesser extent to secondary kin. As far as non-kin are concerned, most evidence suggests that middle-class friendships tend to be less close-knit than their working-class equivalents. This of course is only a general tendency. It seems likely that many middle-class friendship networks contain cliques or clusters of people who are all friends with one another, the more so the more settled in terms of occupational and geographical mobility are the individuals concerned. Conversely, it is clearly mistaken to assume that a majority of working-class people are members of close-knit networks. The image of the working class being embedded in a set of interlocking primary relationships based on kinship, occupation and neighbourhood was shown in Capter 6 to be questionable. None the less, it was suggested there that working-class sociability tends to be context-specific so that consequently working-class males especially are not infrequently members of a recognised set or group of people who all have a similar relationship with one another. As with siblings, we would expect Kapferer's thesis to hold in such cases and for the individuals involved to be constrained by the very fact that these relationships have a group structure. Each will be aware that whatever happens in one relationship will potentially have repercussions in the others. We would therefore expect such relationships to be relatively enduring and stable, as indeed they appear to be. However, we must bear in mind that such clusters of relationships constrain their members more effectively the more significant to the individual each relationship is. That is, when in Kapferer's terms relationships are 'intimate', by which he means 'instrumental in content and many stranded', they bind the individual more strongly than when they are merely 'sociational' (1972, p. 97). As we saw in Chapter 6, most working-class non-kin sociable relationships tend indeed to be purely sociational – and then within a given context – and thus cannot be characterised as multiplex. The extent to which they constrain and dominate the individual is thus limited; he is tied to them but only within the given sphere. Indeed, if his were not so, these relationships could well be viewed by the individual as constraining and thus not be experienced as pleasurable to the same extent.

In conclusion, it is evident that the contribution of network analysis to our understanding of the structure of sociable relationships is limited. In this respect at least the potential that Pahl (1968), Bell (1971) and others attribute to this approach has not been fulfilled. Certainly the approach can help explain why kin relationships endure and why some configurations of sociability constrain their members more than others. But this seems a relatively small return for a development that was seen to promise so much. One reason why network analysis seems at this stage to disappoint is because too much has been expected of it; it is after all merely 'an orienting statement', not a fully fledged theoretical explanation of social patterns. Another reason more directly pertinent to the present concern is that individuals can exercise a good degree of choice over their sociable relationships, especially their non-kin ones. These relationships, in other words, can be made and unmade with greater ease than most, so that all-embracing structural explanations of their development are somewhat unlikely. For this reason it may well be that the network perspective will prove more useful for analysing situations in which the total set of relationships are given and fixed, as for example in Kapferer's earlier study of the workforce in the cell-room of a Zambian mine, than for examining the properties of more nebulous, context-independent, personal stars and zones. However, as discussed at length above, the most important reason why existing studies of personal networks have contributed relatively little to our knowledge of the structure of sociability is that in the main they overlook differences in the nature of the solidarity relationships involve. Until more sophisticated ways of conceptualising 'links' in networks are developed, the idea that individual relationships are in some uncertain way shaped and constrained by the total set to which they belong will remain merely suggestive without progressing beyond this. Indeed, in this respect it would seem that studies of friendship patterns in particular and sociability in general have more to offer network analysis than the latter has to offer them.

NOTE: CHAPTER 8

1 One set of factors that will not be considered here is personality and character traits. The factors in an individual's psychological make-up that affect his or her patterns of sociability are outside the scope of this book. However, two points are worth noting: (1) much of the research in psychology on friendship formation (see Duck, 1973, for a review of this immense literature) is not relevant to this study, as it is concerned with attraction rather than with different patterns of relationship consequent upon attraction; (2) there is an ever-present danger of tautology. For example, it is evidently circular to 'explain' differences in sociability patterns by reference to extrovert or introvert personalities, if the degree of extroversion or introversion is deduced from differences in patterns of sociability in the first place.

Chapter 9

Conclusion

The most appropriate way to begin summarising the conclusions of·
this book is by examining the modifications necessary to the 'general
thesis' contained in occupational and urban community studies. As
discussed in Chapter 1, this general thesis suggests that while the
middle class form friendships with non-kin others met in a comparatively wide range of contexts, working-class people do not. Their
recorded friendships tend to be restricted to a few specific categories
of other: neighbours, workmates, but principally kin. Although
there is some disagreement about the importance of non-kin neighbours and workmates as sources of friendship in working-class social
life – for example Mogey (1956) and Young and Willmott (1962)
found that a majority of their respondents had no non-kin friends
whereas Stacey's (1960) and Goldthorpe et al.'s (1969) research
suggested a less extreme position – all are agreed that kin generally
play a most significant part. In contrast to this, the role of kin in
middle-class sociable life is generally recognised as being quite
minor.

The picture of middle-class sociability presented in this literature
would seem to be accurate in its essentials. There is no doubt that
primary kin relationships involving middle-class adults remain
extant, but these relationships are rarely seen as equivalent to
friendships. Depending on the individual's circumstances, kin can
be relied on for a variety of services, both material and non-
material, especially when these pertain in some way to family life,
but this does not result in their being central in non-familial matters.
Instead middle-class culture encourages the creation of particularistic friendships with a variety of non-kin, irrespective of the
context in which they originally came to be known. Within the
limitations imposed by existing commitments, relationships with
non-kin who are liked are developed into friendships quite readily
by the middle class. This development and creation of friendships
typically involves 'de-contextualising' relationships so that they are

no longer seen as relevant to only one particular setting or type of activity. Instead the middle class emphasise the peculiarity and special qualities of the relationship over and above the context in which it first occurred by broadening it into other settings, of which the individuals' respective homes are the most important. To a degree the significance of kinship in middle-class sociability is reduced the more because particular non-kin relationships are developed into apparently freely chosen friendships in this way. In comparison kin relationships appear to lie outside the individual's volition, given and fixed by nature, and consequently to be of reduced moment in their patterns of sociability. Before turning to working-class patterns, two points need emphasising. First, it is evident the above does not imply that kin relationships are without all significance in middle-class life. The studies by Bell (1968b) and Firth et al. (1970) clearly demonstrate that this is not the case. The role of middle-class kinship in maintaining the class advantages of its members is especially interesting, though the mechanisms by which this is achieved have not as yet been fully studied. Secondly, it is equally clear that more studies of middle-class friendship are required. In particular, comparative research into the friendship patterns of different sections of the middle class, for example of professionals, managers and lower clerical staff, of Watson's spiralists and burgesses, or more simply of middle-class males and females, would be of great interest.

It is in comparison to middle-class patterns that working-class sociability appears to be kin-dominated. However, this influential image lends itself easily to exaggeration. Not all kin relationships are significant in working-class patterns of sociability, nor is it correct to assume that non-kin ones are all unimportant. This latter assumption arises from an implicit acceptance that middle-class methods of developing non-kin relationships are universally applicable. As discussed at some length in Chapter 6, a good deal of available research can be interpreted as suggesting this is not so. Instead of developing non-kin relationships into acknowledged friendships by 'de-contextualising' them and extending their rules of relevance, it would seem that many working-class non-kin relationships are explicitly and purposefully contained within given settings and contexts. This does not mean they are without any importance to those involved but it does make the label 'friendship' appear inapplicable, for ideally friendships should not be constrained or limited in this manner. Because of this, studies which take their working-class respondents' lack of acknowledged non-kin *friends* to indicate the relative unimportance of non-kin in working-class sociable life are wrong. Indeed working-class non-kin relationships appear to be of reduced significance only because it is uncritically assumed that the typical middle-class manner of organising such relationships is in some sense natural. Conversely, some working-class kin relationships, especially those between mothers and their adult daughters and some siblings, appear the more important precisely because they fit this middle-class model better.

We can note that the tendency to treat the middle-class model of sociability as standard is widespread in the research literature. For example, many discussions of primary groups and relationships are biased in this direction. Notwithstanding Cooley's original formulation (see Lee, 1964), feelings of 'we-ness' or, in Schmalenbach's term, 'communion' (1961) have come to be seen as the key element in the primary group concept. A corollary of this is that a concern with the character of individual relationships has replaced the consideration of collective group behaviour, a tendency stemming in part from the merging of Cooley's term with Tönnies's notion of *Gemeinschaft*. Thus what Bates and Babchuk (1961) term 'the social-psychological dimension' of the primary group concept has come to be emphasised over its 'sociological dimension'. According to these authors, whose work undoubtedly reflects recent usage of the term, the former comprises two elements: (1) positive affect; and (2) a particular orientation towards the other involved. This orientation is non-instrumental, non-constraining and based on a willingness to engage with the others involved in 'a considerable range of activity' (1961, p. 183). As the most easily observed, this last aspect appears to be taken frequently as the most important. Thus the prevailing conceptualisation of 'primary group' reflects middle-class non-kin patterns rather more than working-class ones. Non-kin relationships restricted to specific contexts would appear less 'primary' and consequently less significant from the viewpoint of the observer who uncritically accepts that primary relationships as formulated in the literature are the most rewarding and most desired. Equally, and perhaps even more relevant to present research, those many studies which in a taken-for-granted way use some variation of home entertainment (visiting, having round for a meal, sharing a cup of tea, or what have you) as an indicator of the strength of relationships are guilty of a similar error. They are taking as a yardstick a measure that in fact relates to only one particular way of organising relationships. As discussed earlier, entertaining non-kin in the home is an important mechanism through which the middle class develop their associations into friendships. It provides a means of transcending situational boundaries and demonstrates that a relationship is valued for its own sake. However, working-class non-kin relationships are more likely to be defined in terms of a given social setting, with the rules of relevance applied to them not calling for interaction outside that setting. Thus non-kin, however important to the individual they might be, are rarely entertained in the home, which remains largely the preserve of kin.

It naturally follows that to judge the significance of a relationship by the degree of home entertainment is in such cases inappropriate.

To return to the 'general thesis', the portrayal of working-class sociability in it can be questioned on two principal grounds. First, while working-class respondents, unlike middle-class ones, often regard specific kinsmen as important figures in their sociable lives, this does not mean that all kin, or even all those with a given genealogical relationship, are regarded thus. As with the middle class, most kin are of comparatively little importance. Secondly, the claims that working-class friendships are restricted to neighbours and workmates or that non-kin are unimportant in working-class sociability seem to be mistaken. Various non-kin others are interacted with sociably, but the consequent relationships tend to be defined in terms of specific interactional contexts. They are seen as occurring because people happen to be involved simultaneously in a given pursuit rather than as being arranged for their own sake. Consequently, when for some reason an individual is no longer involved in a particular sociable context, the rationale for the relationships he or she had with other people in this context is removed. It follows that workmates and neighbours are likely to be of more significance in working-class than in middle-class sociability for as a result of these processes working-class sociability tends to be more locality-specific. Equally, and for precisely the same reasons, these neighbour and workmate relationships are not equivalent to middle-class friendships. The very way they are organised precludes them from being regarded as such.

OTHER CONSIDERATIONS

A basic point to make in comparing kin and non-kin relationships is that typically they occupy distinct and separate sectors of any individual's sociable life. That is, apart from certain special ceremonial occasions (engagement parties, weddings, and so on) kin and non-kin, as general categories, are rarely purposefully brought together. This does not mean that they never meet, nor that they do not know one another either personally or by reputation. It is merely to affirm that in the normal run of events they do not often impinge upon one another. The relationships are carried on in relative isolation, the occasions on which they are activated being discrete. This routine separation of kin and non-kin can be seen as a consequence of their being based on essentially different principles. In the main the rationale and purpose behind most non-kin sociability is enjoyment. If these relationships are not found enjoyable, interaction is likely to cease. This is not so to the same extent with kin relationships. As shown in Chapter 7, enjoyment is generally not considered particularly relevant to them. Maintaining the blood tie as an on-going relationship is an end in itself, one facilitated by the network characteristic of genealogies. So as well as involving kin, kin meetings are to a great extent *about* kin, kinship being as much a topic of the interaction as a cause of it.

To say that kin and non-kin are generally kept separate from one another does not imply that they never provide similar services or perform equivalent functions to one another in our culture, though it does mean that in any given circumstances an individual is likely to turn to either kin or non-kin, but not both, to achieve his or her particular goals. None the less a number of writers do assume that kin and non-kin provide distinct services from one another, a notable example being Litwak and Szelenyi's work on 'primary group structures' (1969). They are concerned with the structural features that affect the type of assistance that can be given to any individual by various categories of other, especially kin, neighbours and friends. They suggest that neighbours are most capable of immediate, idiosyncratic action (e.g. looking after the children while one runs down to the shops); kin can perform tasks which require long-term ties, (e.g. care during long-term illness); while friends can be relied on for those tasks which require the closest manifest agreement but relatively long-term involvement, (e.g. the creation and maintenance of particular attitudes and values).

Any set of propositions such as these is bound to be of limited value empirically. The assumption that people labelled in a particular way necessarily have a given type of relationship and provide a specific form of service is too rigid. For example, consider first working-class sociability. Not only is friendship as such rare but mates and other non-kin associates are generally defined in a way that limits their influence. Equally in many cases particular kin (because they are neighbours) can be relied on for short-term as well as long-term assistance and (because they are friends) can perform tasks that require agreement and long-term involvement. Similarly non-kin neighbours may provide immediate, idiosyncratic aid but only if there are no kin available, and if they do so it is likely to be on a regular, long-term basis. (Mrs Knowles's dependence on Mrs Clegg is an extreme example of this; see Chapter 6.) In other words it is not neighbours as a category who are relied on but particular neighbours who have developed a sufficiently close relationship. This latter point applies to the middle class too, only in their case the situation is qualified by the way they develop the relationships. The neighbours on whom they rely to perform immediate, idiosyncratic activities will be friends. They are unlikely to have a relationship they could use instrumentally without broadening and developing it into one of friendship in the way outlined in Chapter 5.

So not only do schemas like Litwak and Szelenyi's ignore class-based differences in the organisation of sociability but their basic premise that kin, friends and neighbours provide distinct and separate types of service is too deterministic. Certainly kin and non-kin tend to be kept separate but this does not inevitably mean they perform discrete functions in the way Litwak and Szelenyi imply. At best 'primary group structures' – though 'distance' and 'mobility' may be more appropriate here – impose some limitations on the form relationships can take, but the role of the actors in constructing the rules of relevance of the relationships they have seems equally important.

It is not only in the potential services they provide that kin and non-kin have elements in common. The way these two sets of relationships are developed in working-class sociability, for example, demonstrates an interesting convergence in that interaction in both is frequently seen as contingent rather than organised. That is, what was termed 'structured chance' in Chapter 7 applies, to a degree, to working-class non-kin sociable relationships as well as kin ones. The majority of their non-kin sociable associates are seen in quite bounded settings, with the relationships tending to be defined as consequential on both parties' 'just happening' to be in the same place at the same time. Middle-class non-kin sociability does not share this feature with kinship, being defined as more context-free. Interaction is here conceived of as consequential on planning and purposeful organisation by those involved. But if the majority of working-class non-kin sociable relationships have the above element in common with kin relationships, conversely, (if the Selden Hey respondents are at all typical) 'special' sibling relationships are similar to non-kin relationships in that they involve enjoyment. Maintaining contact is not an end in itself; the emphasis is placed more firmly on compatibility and liking. These kin are friends in the full meaning of the term, and not simply kin.

Just as these kin relationships approach non-kin ones, so some non-kin relationships approach kin. The more non-kin are thought of and labelled 'true friends', the more the symbolism of kinship is used to describe them. There are two elements in particular to this. First, these relationships are often thought to be inalienable for although there is no physical equivalent, like ties based on blood they are unbreakable. Secondly, while enjoyment of interaction remains important, in true friendship trust and shared knowledge also enter the picture – or at least are emphasised more and more. In Bates's terms, the true friends are allowed, reciprocally, an increasingly complete knowledge of all the rooms of the other's house (Bates, 1964). In this they approach aspects of some primary kin relationships, because while most people attempt to keep at least part of their inner selves secret from the majority of their primary kin and would by no means reveal to them every aspect of their life, these kin often know – or imagine they know – what the individual is really like. This knowledge is built up and assumed through shared upbringing and legitimately maintained because in many ways primary kin are conceived of as forming a moral unit. That is, not only are these kin thought of as inalienable, but also to a degree they are seen as responsible for and to one another and can, if necessary, turn (though perhaps return is more appropriate) to each other for support and comfort. This is manifested most in personal crises when it is these kin who are relied upon most often and who will defend most strongly. In this they are the prototype of Cooley's primary group. Of non-kin, only true friends can be relied upon to the same extent. As many folk tales and sayings testify, crisis is the crux of real friendship, the assumption being that at such times only the few – the real and true friends – will remain loyal.

Appendix

Social Class and Patterns of Sociability

Sociologists are frequently accused of being overconcerned with social stratification in general and social class in particular. At times the very parameters of the subject seem to be drawn around a constant examining of the implications and consequences of structured material inequalities. If this were not bad enough, in much empirical sociology, dubious assumptions are made about the existence of distinct classes and about where the boundaries between different classes should be drawn. In particular, the frequent use of the Registrar-General's simplified socio-economic categories for assigning real live people to a position in the class structure denies the variation and range in behaviour and ideology which common experience repeatedly demonstrates. This practice is not made any the more convincing by the recognition – indeed insistence – in theoretical treatises that class structure is inevitably far more complex and intricate than the Registrar-General's scheme implies.

Less justifiable still is the dichotomous operationalisation of social class used in most studies of sociability, including the present one. Deciding a family's class on the criterion of whether the male head of the household is employed manually or non-manually is certainly questionable on a number of grounds. Many would argue it is too simple and too deterministic a model. For example, its disregard of female employment as a factor capable of affecting a family's position in the class structure is clearly debatable. Most important, it separates the population rather too neatly into distinct sectors, almost inevitably encouraging the view that working-class and middle-class life are mutually exclusive. It is as if the population consisted of two separate tribes, the natives of whom not only have different work experiences but also different attitudes, values and beliefs. That is, by oversimplifying the class structure, the manual/non-manual schema implicitly leads towards a 'two-culture' model of society – working-class culture and middle-class culture. The more realistic thesis that both merely represent variations of a single dominant culture is undermined by the tendency inherent in all dichotomous constructions to emphasise diversity at the expense of similarity.

Why, then, given these difficulties, has the manual/non-manual schema been used in the present study? The most obvious (though least satisfactory) answer is that this is the means by which virtually all previous research into patterns of sociability has been analysed. Any report such as this which is concerned with evaluating and developing previous research is inevitably constrained by this practice, for it is impossible to reclassify the data without fuller information than is provided in the published monographs. Similarly, any new material needs to be compatible with the established research if their findings are to be comparable.

This is clearly not an adequate answer to the question posed at the beginning of the last paragraph. Precedence alone can never justify continuing a bad practice, if it so be. There are two parts to a more satisfactory answer. The first concerns the general aptness of a class-based analysis of sociability patterns. Here the proof of the pudding lies in its eating. The essential fact is that in this context class works: it successfully differentiates important variations in the way patterns of sociability are arranged. The consistency with which the 'general thesis' is supported in empirical studies attests to this, the more so as such uniformity is rare in sociology. To argue that class-based differences are real and important does not of course mean that other variables, such as age, religion, geographical factors and, especially, gender, are of no consequence. Clearly they are, but all the available empirical evidence would suggest that they do not shape sociability – or most other aspects of social life – as much as class does.

The second part of the answer revolves around the way social class is operationalised. Even if class is accepted as being the key variable, is it really sensible to operationalise it in terms of a two-tier model based on the type of employment engaged in by the dominant male? The first point to make is that the scale of most research into sociable relationships is such that the concept 'class' inevitably has to be simplified – perhaps to the extent of over-simplification. For example, in the Selden Hey research the size and composition of the sample made anything except a dichotomous classification of class impracticable. This is true for most other studies too. Given this, the manual/non-manual division is without doubt the most appropriate. Clearly there are difficulties with it – by definition there are with any simplification. As recent research on social mobility has demonstrated, in the marginal areas – at the borders of the non-manual/manual categories – there is a good deal of intra-generational mobility backwards and forwards between the two categories. It would be silly to suppose the life style of those concerned alters significantly with each backward or forward move. Equally it is evident that this simplified model does ignore the role of women in the economy. As well as creating difficulties for the classification of fatherless housesholds, it assumes that female labour is peripheral to a family's class location. These and similar criticisms are perfectly valid and raise problems that can only be handled in an arbitrary fashion by the manual/non-manual schema. None the less, given that any way of classifying class structure inevitably simplifies it, the essential point remains that the manual/non-manual simplification is the most pertinent and realistic one. It is without doubt the most important break and natural division within the British class structure. As Parkin notes, 'the fact that we do speak of a class system suggests that we can distinguish some significant "break" in the reward hierarchy. In Western capitalist societies, this line of cleavage falls between the manual and non-manual occupational categories. The logic behind this claim is that differences in the reward position of white-collar or non-manual groups are less marked than are the similarities, when compared with the situation of blue-collar or manual categories' (1972, pp. 24–5). Similarly the nature of male employment is, for better or worse, a more reliable (and conceptually simpler) indicator of a family's economic circumstances and life-style than anything based on female employment.

The claim here then is that while by no means perfect and with all its acknowledged imperfections, the manual/non-manual division is the most appropriate one for our purposes. As well as providing a simplified model by means of which differences in patterns of sociability can be examined, it accurately reflects the essential feature of class structure in our society. It is important to note that a 'two-tribe' or 'two-culture' model of society does not inevitably follow from this. Consistent differences in sociability patterns can be analysed without making the assumption that all aspects of social life are distinct, though this is indeed an inherent danger. Because of the arbitarary and vague nature of the concept 'culture', attempting to specify precise cultural boundaries between groups embedded in a single social structure is as foolhardy as it is complex. It is far better to regard the people involved as members of the same dominant culture whose social practice varies in specifiable ways. Such a formulation also protects us from the folly of supposing that differences between classes are merely differences in socialisation. It forces us to recognise that the middle class and working class are not completely independent and isolated from each other, and consequently encourages us to specify why such differences as exist arise. In the end it is not sufficient merely to assert that class is the key variable; the links between different people's material circumstances and their social habits also need to be examined. A start in this direction has been made in various sections of this book, especially in Chapters 6 and 8, although throughout the main emphasis has of course been on the logically prior task of specifying more adequately the main patterns of sociability found empirically.

Bibliography

Adams, B. N., 'The middle-class adult and his widowed or still-married mother', *Social Problems*, vol. 16 (1965), pp. 50-9.

Adams, B. N., 'Interaction theory and the social network', *Sociometry*, vol. 30 (1967), pp. 64-78.

Adams, B. N., *Kinship in an Urban Setting* (Chicago: Markham, 1968).

Adams, B. N., 'Isolation, function and beyond: American kinship in the 1960s', *Journal of Marriage and the Family*, vol. 32 (1970), pp. 575-97.

Adams, B. N., 'The social significance of kinship', in *Sociology of the Family*, ed. M. Anderson (Harmondsworth: Penguin Books, 1971), pp. 126-41.

Allan, G. A., 'Friendship and kinship' (unpublished PhD thesis, University of Essex, 1976).

Allan, G. A., 'Sibling solidarity', *Journal of Marriage and the Family*, vol. 39 (1977), pp. 177-84.

Allan, G. A., 'Class variations in friendship patterns', *British Journal of Sociology*, vol. 28 (1977), pp. 389-93.

Allan, G. A., 'A note on interviewing spouses together', *Journal of Marriage and the Family*, in press.

Allcorn, D. H., and Marsh, C. M., 'Occupational communities – communities of what?', in *Working Class Images of Society*, ed. M. Bulmer (London: Routledge & Kegan Paul, 1975), pp. 206-18.

Anderson, M. (ed.), *Sociology of the Family* (Harmondsworth: Penguin Books, 1971).

Aronson, D. R., 'Social networks: towards structure or process?', *Canadian Review of Sociology and Anthropology*, vol. 7 (1970), pp. 258-68.

Babchuck, N., 'Primary friends and kin: a study of the associations of middle class couples', *Social Forces*, vol. 43 (1965), pp. 483-93.

Babchuk, N., and Bates, A., 'The primary relations of middle class couples: a study of male dominance', *American Sociological Review*, vol. 28 (1963), pp. 377-91.

Banton, M., *The Social Anthropology of Complex Societies* (London: Tavistock, 1966).

Barker, D. L., 'Young people and their homes: spoiling and "keeping close" in a South Wales town', *Sociological Review*, vol. 20 (1972), pp. 569-90.

Barker, D. L., and Allen, S., (eds), *Dependence and Exploitation in Work and Marriage* (London, Longman, 1976).

Barnes, J. A., 'Class and committees in a Norwegian island parish', *Human Relations*, vol. 7 (1954), pp. 39-58.

Barnes, J. A., 'Physical and social kinship', *Philosophy of Science*, vol. 28 (1961), pp. 296-9.

Barnes, J. A., 'Physical and social facts in anthropology', *Philosophy of Science*, vol. 31 (1964), pp. 294-7.

Barnes, J. A., 'Genealogies', in *The Craft of Social Anthropology*, ed. A. L. Epstein (London: Tavistock, 1967), pp. 101-27.

Barnes, J. A., 'Networks and political process', in *Social Networks in Urban Situations*, ed. J. C. Mitchell (Manchester: Manchester University Press, 1969), pp. 51-76.

Barnes, J. A., 'Social networks', *Module in Anthropology*, No. 26 (Reading, Mass.: Addison-Wesley, 1972).

Barth, F., *Models of Social Organization*, Occasional Papers of the Royal Anthropological Institute, No. 23 (London: Royal Anthropological Institute, 1966).

Bates, A., 'Privacy – a useful concept?', *Social Forces*, vol. 42 (1964), pp. 429–34.

Bates, A., and Babchuk, N., 'The primary group: a re-appraisal', *Sociological Quarterly*, vol. 2 (1961), pp. 181–91.

Beattie, J. H. M., 'Kinship and social anthropology', *Man*, vol. 64 (1964), pp. 101–3.

Bell, C. R., 'Mobility and the middle class extended family', *Sociology*, vol. 2 (1968a), pp. 173–84.

Bell, C. R., *Middle Class Families* (London: Routledge & Kegan Paul, 1968b).

Bell, C. R., review of Firth *et al.* (1970) and Schneider (1968), *Sociology*, vol. 5 (1971), pp. 130–3.

Bell, C. R., 'Occupational career, family cycle and extended family relations', *Human Relations*, vol. 24 (1972), pp. 463–75.

Bell, W., and Boat, M., 'Urban neighbourhoods and informal social relations', *American Journal of Sociology*, vol. 62 (1957) pp. 391–8.

Berger, P. L., and Luckmann, T., *The Social Construction of Reality* (Garden City, New York: Doubleday Anchor, 1967).

Bernstein, B., *Class, Codes and Control*, Vol. 1 (London: Paladin, 1973).

Birch, A. H., *Small Town Politics* (London: OUP, 1959).

Blau, P. M., *Exchange and Power in Social Life* (New York: Wiley, 1964).

Blau, Z., 'Structural constraints on friendship in old age', *American Sociological Review*, vol. 26 (1961), pp. 429–39.

Blauner, R., 'Work satisfaction and industrial trends in modern society', in *Labour and Trade Unionism*, ed. W. Galenson and S. M. Lipset (New York: Wiley, 1960), pp. 339–60.

Blum, A. F., 'Social structure, social class and participation in primary relationships', in *Blue-Collar World: Studies of the American Worker*, ed. A. B. Shostak and W. Gomberg (Englewood Cliffs, NJ: Prentice-Hall, 1964), pp. 195–207.

Boissevain, J., *Friends of Friends* (Oxford: Blackwell, 1974).

Boissevain, J., and Mitchell, J. C., *Network Analysis: Studies in Human Interaction* (The Hague: Mouton, 1973).

Booth, A., and Hess, E., 'Cross sexual friendships', *Journal of Marriage and the Family*, vol. 36 (1974), pp. 38–47.

Boswell, D., 'Kinship, friendship and the concept of social network', *Proceedings of the East African Institute of Social Research*, no. 379 (1966).

Bott, E., *Family and Social Network* (London: Tavistock, 1957, 1971).

Brain, R., *Friends and Lovers* (London: Hart-Davis, MacGibbon, 1976).

Brown, R. K., Brannen, P., Cousins, J. M., and Samphier, M. L., 'The contours of solidarity: social stratification and industrial relations in shipbuilding', *British Journal of Industrial Relations*, vol. 10 (1972), pp. 12–41.

Brown, R. K., Brannen, P., Cousins, J. M., and Samphier, M. L., 'Leisure in work: the "occupational culture" of shipbuilding workers', in *Leisure and Society in Britain*, ed. M. A. Smith, S. Parker and C. Smith (London: Allen Lane, 1973), pp. 97–110.

Bulmer, M. (ed.), *Working Class Images of Society* (London: Routledge & Kegan Paul, 1975).

Burns, T., 'Friends, enemies and the polite fiction', *American Sociological Review*, vol. 18 (1953), pp. 654–62.

Burridge, K., 'Friendship in Tangu', *Oceania*, vol. 27 (1957), pp. 177–89.

Chambliss, W. J., 'The selection of friends', *Social Forces*, vol. 43 (1965), pp. 370–80.

Cohen, Y., 'Patterns of friendship', in *Social Structure and Personality*, ed. Y. Cohen (New York: Holt, Rinehart & Winston, 1961), pp. 351–86.
Cooley, C. H., *Social Organization* (New York: Schocken, 1962).
Cousins, J. M., and Brown, R. K., 'Patterns of paradox: shipbuilding workers' images of society', in *Working Class Images of Society*, ed. M. Bulmer (London: Routledge & Kegan Paul, 1975).
Cubitt, T., 'Network density among urban families' in *Network Analysis: Studies in Human Interaction*, ed. J. Boissevain and J. C. Mitchell (The Hague: Mouton, 1973), pp. 67–82.
Cumming, E., and Henry, W. F., *Growing Old: The Process of Disengagement* (New York: Basic Books, 1961).
Cumming, E., and Schneider, D., 'Sibling solidarity: a property of American kinship', *American Anthropologist*, vol. 63 (1961), pp. 498–507.
Davis, J., 'Forms and norms: the economy of social relations', *Man* (n.s.), vol. 8 (1973), pp. 159–76.
Dennis, N., Henriques, F., and Slaughter, C., *Coal is Our Life* (London: Tavistock, 1956).
Duck, S., *Personal Relationships and Personal Constructs* (London: Wiley, 1973).
Edgell, S., 'Friendship patterns and the life cycle' (unpublished manuscript, n.d.).
Edwards, J. N., 'Familial behaviour as social exchange', *Journal of Marriage and the Family*, vol. 31 (1969), pp. 518–26.
Eisenstadt, S. N., 'Ritualized personal relations', *Man*, vol. 56, no. 96 (1956).
Elias, N., 'Towards a theory of communities', in *The Sociology of Community*, ed. C. Bell and H. Newby (London: Cass, 1973), pp. ix–xli.
Epstein, A. L., 'The network and urban social organization', in *Social Networks in Urban Situations*, ed. J. C. Mitchell (Manchester: Manchester University Press, 1969), pp. 77–116.
Fallding, H., 'The family and the idea of a cardinal role', *Human Relations*, vol. 14 (1961), pp. 329–50.
Faris, E., 'The primary group: essence and accident', *American Journal of Sociology*, vol. 37 (1932), pp. 41–50.
Fellin, P., and Litwak, E., 'Neighbourhood cohesion under conditions of mobility', *American Sociological Review*, vol. 28 (1963), pp. 364–76.
Firth, R., *Two Studies of Kinship in London*, (London: Athlone, 1956).
Firth, R., 'Family and kin ties in Britain and their social implications', *British Journal of Sociology*, vol. 12 (1961), pp. 305–10.
Firth, R., Hubert, J., and Forge, A., *Families and their Relatives* (Routledge & Kegan Paul, 1970).
Frankenberg, R., *Village on the Border* (London: Cohen & West, 1957).
Frankenberg, R., *Communities in Britain* (Harmondsworth: Penguin Books, 1969).
Gans, H. J., *The Levittowners* (London: Allen Lane, 1967).
Gans, H. J., 'Urbanism and suburbanism as ways of life', in *Readings in Urban Sociology*, ed. R. Pahl (Oxford: Pergamon, 1968), pp. 95–118.
Gavron, H., *The Captive Wife* (Harmondsworth: Penguin Books, 1966).
Gellner, E., 'Ideal language and kinship structure', *Philosophy of Science*, vol. 24 (1957), pp. 235–43.
Gellner, E., 'The concept of kinship', *Philosophy of Science*, vol. 27 (1960), pp. 187–204.
Gellner, E., 'Nature and society in social anthropology', *Philosophy of Science*, vol. 30 (1963), pp. 236–51.
Ghurye, G. S., 'Friendship as a category of social relations', *Sociological Bulletin*, vol. 2 (1953), pp. 143–60.
Goffman, E., *The Presentation of Self in Everyday Life* (Garden City, New York: Doubleday Anchor, 1959).

Goldthorpe, J., Lockwood, D., Bechhofer, F., and Platt, J., *The Affluent Worker in the Class Structure* (Cambridge: CUP, 1969).

Halsey, A. H. (ed.), *Trends in British Society Since 1900* (London: Macmillan, 1972).

Harrell-Bond, B. E., 'Conjugal role behaviour', *Human Relations*, vol. 22 (1969), pp. 77–91.

Harris, C. C., *The Family* (London: Allen & Unwin, 1969).

Hill, S., *The Dockers* (London: Heinemann, 1976).

Hodges, M. W., and Smith, C., 'The Sheffield estate', in *Neighbourhood and Community*, ed. T. Simey (Liverpool: Liverpool University Press, 1954).

Hollowell, P. G., *The Lorry Driver* (London: Routledge & Kegan Paul, 1968).

Kapferer, B., 'Norms and the manipulation of relationships in a work context', in *Social Networks in Urban Situations*, ed. J. C. Mitchell (Manchester: Manchester University Press, 1969), pp. 181–244.

Kapferer, B., 'Social network and conjugal role in Zambia', in *Network Analysis: Studies in Social Interaction*, ed. J. Boissevain and J. C. Mitchell (The Hague: Mountin, 1973), pp. 83–110.

Keesing, R. M., 'Simple models of complexity: the lure of kinship', in *Kinship Studies in the Morgan Centennial Year*, ed. P. Reining (Washington, DC: Washington Anthropological Society, 1972), pp. 17–31.

Kerr, M., *The People of Ship Street* (London: Routledge & Kegan Paul, 1958).

Klein, J., *Samples from English Culture* (London: Routledge & Kegan Paul, 1965).

Kurth, S., 'Friendships and friendly relations', in *Social Relationships*, ed. G. McCall (Chicago: Aldine, 1970), pp. 136–69.

Lancaster, L., 'Some conceptual problems in the study of family and kin ties in the British Isles', *British Journal of Sociology*, vol. 12 (1961), pp. 317–33.

Lazarsfeld, P. and Merton, R., 'Friendship as social process', in *Freedom and Control in Modern Society*, ed. M. Berger, T. Abel and C. H. Page, (Princeton, NJ: Van Nostrand, 1954), pp. 18–66.

Lee, S. C., 'The primary group as Cooley defines it', *Sociological Quarterly*, vol. 5 (1964), pp. 23–34.

Lewis, C. S., *The Four Loves* (London: Geoffrey Bles, 1960).

Leyton, E., *The Compact* (Newfoundland Social and Economic Papers No. 3: Memorial University of Newfoundland, 1974).

Liebow, E., *Tally's Corner* (Boston, Mass.: Little, Brown, 1967).

Linton, R., *The Study of Man* (New York: Appleton-Century 1963).

Littlejohn, J., *Westrigg* (London: Routledge & Kegan Paul, 1963).

Litwak, E., 'Occupational mobility and extended family cohesion', *American Sociological Review*, vol. 25 (1960a), pp. 9–21.

Litwak, E., 'Geographic mobility and extended family cohesion', *American Sociological Review*, vol. 25 (1960b), pp. 385–94.

Litwak, E., 'Extended kin relations in an industrial democratic society', in *Social Structure and the Family*, ed. E. Shanas and G. F. Streib (Englewood Cliffs, NJ: Prentice-Hall, 1965), pp. 290–323.

Litwak, E., and Szelenyi, I., 'Primary group structures and their functions: kin, neighbours and friends', *American Sociological Review*, vol. 34 (1969), pp. 465–81.

Lockwood, D., 'Sources of variation in working class images of society', *Sociological Review*, vol. 14 (1966), pp. 249–67.

Lupton, T., and Mitchell, G. D., 'The Liverpool estate' in *Neighbourhood and Community*, ed. T. Simey (Liverpool: Liverpool University Press, 1954).

Lupton, T., and Wilson, C. S., 'The social background and connections of "top decision-makers" ', *The Manchester School*, vol. 27 (1959), pp. 30–51.

Marris, P., *Widows and their Families* (London: Routledge & Kegan Paul, 1958).

Mayer, A. C., 'The significance of quasi-groups in the study of complex societies', in *The Social Anthropology of Complex Societies*, ed. M. Banton (London: Tavistock, 1966), pp. 97–122.

McCall, G., Denzin, N., Kurth, S., McCall, M., and Suttles, G., 'A collaborative overview of social relationships', in *Social Relationships*, ed. G. McCall (Chicago: Aldine, 1970), pp. 171–82.

McCall, G. (ed.), *Social Relationships* (Chicago: Aldine, 1970).

Mitchell, J. C. (ed.), *Social Networks in Urban Situations* (Manchester: Manchester University Press, 1969).

Mitchell, J. C., 'Networks, norms and institutions', in *Network Analysis: Studies in Human Interaction*, ed. J. Boissevain and J. C. Mitchell (The Hague: Mouton, 1973), pp. 15–35.

Mogey, J., *Family and Neighbourhood* (London: OUP, 1956).

Moore, R. S., 'Religion as a source of variation in working class images of society', in *Working Class Images of Society*, ed. M. Bulmer (London: Routledge & Kegan Paul, 1975), pp. 35–54.

Morgan, D. H. J., *Social Theory and the Family* (London: Routledge & Kegan Paul, 1975).

Naegale, K., 'Friendship and acquaintances: an exploration of some social distinctions', *Harvard Educational Review*, vol. 28 (1958), pp. 232–52.

Needham, R., 'Descent systems and ideal language', *Philosophy of Science*, vol. 27 (1960), pp. 96–101.

Oakley, A., *The Sociology of Housework* (London: Martin Robertson, 1974).

Oxley, H. G., *Mateship and Local Organization* (Brisbane: University of Queensland Press, 1974).

Pahl, J. M., and Pahl, R. E., *Managers and their Wives* (Harmondsworth: Penguin Books, 1971).

Pahl, R. E., 'The rural-urban continuum', in *Readings in Urban Sociology*, ed. R. Pahl (Oxford: Pergamon, 1968), pp. 263–97.

Pahl, R. E., 'A sociological portrait: friends and associates', *New Society*, vol. 18 (1971), pp. 980–2.

Paine, R., 'In search of friendship', *Man* (n.s.), vol. 4 (1969), pp. 505–24.

Paine, R., 'Anthropological approaches to friendship', *Humanitas*, vol. 6 (1970), pp. 139–59. (Also in E. Leyton, 1974.)

Parker, S., *The Sociology of Leisure* (London: Allen & Unwin, 1976).

Parkin, F., *Class Inequality and Political Order* (London: Paladin, 1972).

Pickvance, C. G. (ed.), *Urban Sociology: Critical Essays* (London: Tavistock, 1976).

Pitt-Rivers, J., 'Interpersonal relations in peasant society', *Human Organization*, vol. 19 (1961), pp. 180–3.

Pitt-Rivers, J., *People of the Sierra* (Chicago: Phoenix, 1963).

Platt, J., 'Some problems in measuring the jointness of conjugal role relationships', *Sociology*, vol. 3 (1969), pp. 287–97.

Ramsoy, O., 'Friendship', *International Encyclopaedia of Social Science*, vol. 6 (New York: Macmillan, 1968).

Rapoport, R., and Rapoport, R., *Dual-Career Families* (Harmondsworth: Penguin Books, 1971).

Rapoport, R., and Rapoport, R., *Leisure and the Family Life Cycle* (London: Routledge & Kegan Paul, 1975).

Rapoport, R., and Rapoport, R., *Dual-Career Families Re-examined* (London: Martin Robertson, 1976).

Reina, R., 'Two patterns of friendship in a Guatemalan community', *American Anthropologist*, vol. 61 (1969), pp. 44–50.

Richer, S., 'The economics of child rearing', *Journal of Marriage and the Family*, vol. 30 (1968), pp. 462–6.

Rose, A. M., *Human Behaviour and Social Processes* (London: Routledge & Kegan Paul, 1962).

Rosenberg, G., and Anspach, D., 'Sibling solidarity in the working class', *Journal of Marriage and the Family*, vol. 35 (1973), pp. 108–13.

Rosow, I., 'Old people: their friends and neighbours', *American Behavioural Scientist*, vol. 14 (1970), pp. 59–69.

Rosser, C., and Harris, C., 'Relationships through marriage in a Welsh urban area', *Sociological Review*, vol. 9 (1961), pp. 293–321.

Rosser, C., and Harris, C., *The Family and Social Change* (London: Routledge & Kegan Paul, 1965).

Sadler, W., 'The experience of friendship', *Humanitas*, vol. 6 (1970), pp. 177–209.

Salaman, G., *Community and Occupation*, Cambridge Papers in Sociology No. 4 (Cambridge: CUP, 1974).

Schmalenbach, H., 'The sociological category of communion', in *Theories of Society*, Vol. 1, ed. T. Parsons, E. Shils, K. D. Naegale and J. R. Pitts (Glencoe: The Free Press, 1961), pp. 331–47.

Schneider, D., *American Kinship: A Cultural Account* (Englewood Cliffs, NJ: Prentice-Hall, 1968).

Schneider, D., 'Kinship, religion and nationality', in *Forms of Symbolic Action*, Proceedings of the 1969 Spring Meeting of the American Ethnological Society, ed. V. Turner (Seattle: University of Washington Press, 1969), pp. 116–25.

Schneider, D., 'What is kinship all about?', in *Kinship Studies in the Morgan Centennial Year*, ed. P. Reining (Washington, DC: Washington Anthropological Society, 1972), pp. 32–63.

Schneider, D., and Homans, G., 'Kinship terminology and the American kinship system', *American Anthropologist*, vol. 57 (1955), pp. 1194–208.

Schneider, D., and Smith R., *Class Differences and Sex Roles in American Kinship and Family Structure* (Englewood Cliffs, NJ: Prentice-Hall, 1973).

Seeley, J. R., Sim, A. A., and Loosley, E. W., *Crestwood Heights* (Toronto: University of Toronto Press, 1956).

Shanas, E., and Streib, G. F., *Social Structure and the Family: Generational Relations* (Englewood Cliffs, NJ: Prentice-Hall, 1965).

Shaw, L., 'Impressions of family life in a London suburb', *Sociological Review*, vol. 2 (1954), pp. 179–94.

ıith, M. A., Parker, S., and Smith, C. (eds), *Leisure and Society in Britain* (London: Allen Lane, 1973).

Stacey, M., *Tradition and Change* (London: OUP, 1960).

Stacey, M., Batstone, E., Bell, C., and Murcott, A., *Power, Persistence and Change* (London: Routledge & Kegan Paul, 1975).

Sussman, M. B., 'Relationships of adult children with their parents in the United States', in *Social Structure and the Family: Generational Relations*, ed. E. Shanas and G. F. Streib (Englewood Cliffs, NJ: Prentice-Hall, 1965), pp. 62–92.

Sussman, M. B., and Burchinal, L., 'Kin family network: unheralded structure in current conceptualizations of family functioning', *Marriage and Family Living*, vol. 24 (1962), pp. 231–40.

Sutcliffe, J. P., and Crabbe, B. D., 'Incidence and degrees of friendship in urban and rural areas', *Social Forces*, vol. 42 (1963), pp. 60–7.

Suttles, G., 'Friendship as a social institution', in *Social Relationships*, ed. G. McCall (Chicago: Aldine, 1970), pp. 95–135.

Thorns, D., *Suburbia* (London: MacGibbon & Kee, 1972).

Toomey, D. M., 'Conjugal roles and social networks in an urban working class sample', *Human Relations*, vol. 24 (1971), pp. 417–31.

Townsend, P., *The Family Life of Old People* (Harmondsworth: Penguin Books, 1963).

Tunstall, J., *The Fisherman* (London: MacGibbon & Kee, 1962).

Turner, C., *The Social Anthropology of an Upper Weardale Parish* (unpublished PhD, Durham University, 1964).

Turner, R. H., 'Role-taking: process versus conformity', in *Human Behaviour and Social Processes*, ed. A. M. Rose (London: Routledge & Kegan Paul, 1962), pp. 20–40.

Turner, V., *The Ritual Process* (Harmondsworth: Penguin Books, 1974).

Warner, W. L., and Lunt, P. S., *The Social Life of a Modern Community* (New Haven: Yale University Press, 1959).

Watson, W., 'Social mobility and social class in industrial communities', in *Closed Systems and Open Minds*, ed. M. Gluckman and E. Devons (Edinburgh: Oliver & Boyd, 1964), pp. 129–57.

Wheeldon, P. D., 'The operation of voluntary associations and personal networks in the political processes of an inter-ethnic community', in *Social Networks in Urban Situations*, ed. J. C. Mitchell (Manchester: Manchester University Press, 1969), pp. 128–80.

Whitehead, A., 'Sexual antagonism in Herefordshire', in *Dependence and Exloitation in Work and Marriage*, ed. D. L. Barker and S. Allen (London: Longman, 1976), pp. 169–203.

Whyte, W. F., *Street Corner Society* (Chicago: Chicago University Press, 1943).

Whyte, W. H., *The Organization Man* (Harmondsworth: Penguin Books, 1960).

Williams, R. H., 'Friendship and social values in a suburban community: an exploratory study', *Pacific Sociological Review*, vol. 2 (1959), pp. 3–10.

Williams, W. M., *The Sociology of an English Village: Gosforth* (London: Routedge & Kegan Paul, 1956).

Williams, W. M., *A West Country Village: Ashworthy* (London: Routledge & Kegan Paul, 1963).

Willmott, P., *The Evolution of a Community* (London: Routledge & Kegan Paul, 1963).

Willmott, P., and Young, M., *Family and Class in a London Suburb* (London: Nel Mentor, 1967).

Wirth, L., 'Urbanism as a way of life', *American Journal of Sociology*, vol. 44 (1938), pp. 1–24.

Wolf, E. R., 'Kinship, friendship and patron–client relations in complex societies', in *The Social Anthropology of Complex Societies*, ed. M. Banton (London: Tavistock, 1966), pp. 1–22.

Wolff, K. H., *The Sociology of George Simmel* (New York: The Free Press, 1950).

Worsley, P., *The Trumpet Shall Sound* (London: MacGibbon & Kee, 1968).

Young, M., and Willmott, P., *Family and Kinship in East London* (Harmondsworth: Penguin Books, 1962).

Young, M., and Willmott, P., *The Symmetrical Family* (London: Routledge & Kegan Paul, 1973).

INDEX

For Product Safety Concerns and Information please contact our EU
representative GPSR@taylorandfrancis.com
Taylor & Francis Verlag GmbH, Kaufingerstraße 24, 80331 München, Germany

* 9 7 8 1 0 3 2 1 0 3 7 3 0 *